Also by Terry Pluto

ON SPORTS:

The Browns Blues
The Comeback: LeBron, the Cavs and Cleveland
Glory Days in Tribe Town (with Tom Hamilton)
Joe Tait: It's Been a Real Ball (with Joe Tait)
Things I've Learned from Watching the Browns
LeBron James: The Making of an MVP (with Brian Windhorst)
The Franchise (with Brian Windhorst)
Dealing: The Cleveland Indians' New Ballgame
False Start: How the New Browns Were Set Up to Fail
The View from Pluto
Unguarded (with Lenny Wilkens)
Our Tribe
Browns Town 1964
Burying the Curse
The Curse of Rocky Colavito
Falling from Grace
Tall Tales
Loose Balls
Bull Session (with Johnny Kerr)
Tark (with Jerry Tarkanian)
Forty-Eight Minutes, a Night in the Life of the NBA (with Bob Ryan)
Sixty-One (with Tony Kubek)
You Could Argue But You'd Be Wrong (with Pete Franklin)
Weaver on Strategy (with Earl Weaver)
The Earl of Baltimore
Super Joe (with Joe Charboneau and Burt Graeff)
The Greatest Summer

ON FAITH AND OTHER TOPICS:

Faith and You
Faith and You, Volume 2
Everyday Faith
Champions for Life: The Power of a Father's Blessing (with Bill Glass)
Crime: Our Second Vietnam (with Bill Glass)

Vintage CAVS

A Warm Look Back at the Cavaliers of the Cleveland Arena and Richfield Coliseum Years

TERRY PLUTO

GRAY & COMPANY, PUBLISHERS

CLEVELAND

To Joe Tait,
because you lived it

Gray & Company, Publishers
www.grayco.com

ISBN 978-1-59851-108-6
Printed in the United States of America
1

Contents

Vintage CAVS

About This Book

This book is about the Cavaliers from the days of the old Cleveland Arena and Richfield Coliseum.

It's not meant to be an in-depth history.

It's a personal history. It's about how it felt—not just a cold collection of facts and quotes.

For example, the dismal days of Ted Stepien could be a full book. I give it one chapter. Yes, parts are funny. But it was a time when Northeast Ohio nearly lost the Cavaliers and an entire generation of basketball fans.

If you'd like a thorough history of the Cavaliers with about 100 different subjects interviewed, I recommend "From Fitch to Fratello," written by Joe Menzer and Burt Graeff. Another resource is "The Franchise," written by Brian Windhorst and myself.

I have worked hard to get the facts right. My star researcher Larry Pantages was a huge help in that area.

But this is more memoir and memory—my memories.

Think of it like basketball itself. The game is best played more like jazz than a scripted "hit all the notes right" classic symphony. I grew up watching some Cavs games at the old downtown arena. I covered the Cavaliers from 1985 to 1993 when they played at the Coliseum.

The idea for this book was rattling around in the attic of my mind for years, but I wondered if anyone would want to read it.

But when John "Hot Rod" Williams died in 2015 and I wrote a few stories about him, I was overwhelmed by the response of readers.

Thanks to the Internet, we have a good idea how many people read and connect with certain stories.

Then the challenge became how and when to write the book.

In 2019–20, the Cavaliers are entering their 50th season. Driving past the field where the Cavaliers once played in Richfield convinced me the time was now. Just write the book, ask readers for memories and put it out there.

And that's what I did.

CHAPTER 1

Ghosts

Someone once said, "You know you've reached a certain age when you remember a sports venue being built, and then see the same building torn down."

I think of that when driving down Route 303 in Richfield, at the exit off Interstate 271.

Now, there is nothing but a field bumping up against some nearby farms and barns. Staring at it, there's a sense it has been and will always be like this—a quiet spot that time forgot.

But once upon a time, a great arena rose up among the trees and squirrels and deer and prairie grass. For a while, it was a sports palace right next to a guy's farm with sheep grazing on it.

The Richfield Coliseum.

Long gone.

But I close my eyes and I hear the booming voice of the late Howie Chizek proclaiming: 'WORLD . . . BEE . . . FREE . . . FOR THAA . . . REE!!!"

I'm sure there have been better pro basketball public address announcers than Chizek, but I never heard one.

How about: "WHAM WITH THE RIGHT HAND!"

Maybe there have been better pro basketball radio broadcasters than Joe Tait, but I never heard one.

And while there is no denying the LeBron James teams were the best in Cleveland Cavalier history, I don't find myself drawn to them the way I am to earlier Cavs teams.

I think of World B. Free, who averaged 23 points a game for the Cavaliers from 1982 to 1986. We became friends when I covered the Cavs for the Akron Beacon Journal in 1985–86, his final season. After practice, we would play a game of 3-point H-O-R-S-E.

You had to take 3-point shots from different spots behind the arc. If Free made a shot and I missed, I got a letter. An H . . .

Every time that happened, another letter. To make it fair, Free said I only needed to hang one letter on him. In other words, if I made one shot and he missed, he had all five letters—H-O-R-S-E.

Some of our games took a half-hour, but he never lost. He could make 10 in a row from 5-to-10 feet behind the arc. This was long before the 3-pointer became the favored shot as it is today.

But that court and those baskets are long gone.

So is the time when writers could watch practice and then be invited by a player to shoot around after it was over.

All that's left is a field. Not a field of dreams—just a memory on the edge of a national park between Cleveland and Akron.

Once, on a visit to Cleveland, Free had a cab driver take him from downtown to where the Coliseum once ruled. He stood and stared at the field. So many memories, so lost in time.

Sometimes, I'm the same way.

Staring . . .

Thinking . . .

Hearing the squeaking of the shoes over the roar of the crowd— because sports writers sat near the court in those days.

The wind blows through leaves, the prairie grass bends in the breeze . . .

Mark Price . . . Austin Carr . . . Larry Nance Sr. . . . Brad Daugherty . . . Hot Rod Williams . . . Ron Harper . . . Lenny Wilkens . . . Bingo Smith . . . Campy Russell . . . Nate Thurmond . . . Jim Chones.

They hung no title banners. Some seasons, they lost far more than they won.

But they were my Cavaliers.

I've been writing about sports long enough to know there never was an age of innocence. What seems like small change now,

Where the 20,000-seat Richfield Coliseum once stood is now a field in the Cuyahoga Valley National Park. This view (top) is from Rt. 303 looking north from what used to be (approximately) the east driveway entrance to the Coliseum. *Top: Chris Stephens / The Plain Dealer. Bottom: Gus Chan / The Plain Dealer*

looking in the rear view mirror of life, seemed like big dollars at the time.

The love of the game and the love of money have always been in a spiritual tug-of-war for those involved in pro sports. There have always been deal makers, liars, egotists and cravers of publicity involved with the Cavaliers.

That said, it was a different game when the Cavaliers were born in 1970. They played at the smoky, dumpy old Cleveland Arena on Euclid Avenue for their first four years.

And it was a different game when the team moved to Richfield in 1974.

And I maintain, it was a better game—or at least more of a game than what we see now in the NBA.

I write this knowing none of the Cavs teams playing at the old Cleveland Arena or Richfield Coliseum even reached the NBA Finals, much less won a title.

I write this knowing the Cavs did win the 2016 title—with LeBron James—at what was then called Quicken Loans Arena in downtown Cleveland.

For many Cleveland sports fans, recalling Fathers' Day of June 19, 2016, will bring tears to their eyes as they remember dancing in the streets of downtown Cleveland after the Cavs came back from a 3-1 deficit to beat Golden State in Game 7 of the NBA Finals.

It remains the greatest comeback in NBA Finals history. It is the most amazing sports event that I ever covered, keeping in mind the game was played at Oracle Arena in Oakland.

But I also write this knowing a lot of the details of what it took to deliver that title—the first for a major Cleveland sports franchise since the 1964 Browns.

It was a marriage of convenience between two men who couldn't stand each other. It was like a major corporate merger, two of the most powerful people in the NBA.

No NBA player had made more money or had more influence than LeBron James, when he left the Miami Heat for the Cavaliers in the summer of 2014. And no Cleveland sports owner was willing to spend more money to win a title than Dan Gilbert.

While the two men barely spoke in those four seasons (2014-18), the Cavs went to the NBA Finals four times. It was purely a cold-hearted, bottom-line business proposition that paid off for both parties—and for Cleveland sports fans.

But that also was a different game, as I wrote in my book "The Comeback." I used to think Michael Jordan was the greatest player

I've ever seen—and that included Jerry West, Bill Russell, Wilt Chamberlain, Larry Bird and Magic Johnson.

Now, LeBron James would get that vote from me because of all he did to win a title in Cleveland. And Dan Gilbert deserves credit for putting things in place to make that happen.

So none of what I write here is meant to diminish the accomplishments of those two men and the Cavs from 2014 to 2018. In sports, the bottom line is winning—and they won more than anyone else in Cavs history.

Yet, I'm drawn to the Cavaliers before LeBron James . . .

Before Quicken Loans Arena . . .

Before so much of basketball was about who was leaving as a free agent and where that player would land in the summer . . .

It was Lenny Wilkens drawing up beautiful in-bounds plays . . .

Bill Fitch screaming at Jim Chones . . .

Mark Price and Brad Daugherty giving a clinic on pick-and-roll plays . . .

And the memory of an arena long gone, but so alive in my mind.

CHAPTER 2

An Old Program

The program is only four pages. It's more than 50 years old.

On the cover is a picture of Oscar Robertson dribbling a basketball. The headline reads: CINCINNATI ROYALS BASKETBALL, 1969–70.

There are small advertisements for Paramount Distillers and Black Label Beer.

The bottom of the cover reads: Sponsored by the Cleveland Browns and the Cleveland Plain Dealer . . . CLEVELAND ARENA

The program was for a Nov. 28, 1969, game between the Cincinnati Royals and New York Knicks.

On the two inside pages are the rosters for both teams, and two huge advertisements:

SOME VODKAS ARE BETTER THAN OTHERS . . . PARAMOUNT IS SOME VODKA!

WORLD CHAMPION . . . BLACK LABEL BEER.

Apparently, some people believed the best way to digest pro basketball in that old Cleveland Arena on Euclid Avenue between East 36th and East 40th streets was with a stiff drink—or maybe more than a few.

Right next door to the old Arena for years on Euclid Avenue was a place called the Sportsman Lounge. Back then, a lot of Cleveland fans drank—and were apparently very proud of it!

The author's program from the Nov. 28, 1969, Cincinnati Royals game at the Cleveland Arena—with autographs. *Author's collection*

By 1969, the Cleveland Arena was 32 years old—and it felt and looked much older. But what did I know? It was the only place where I'd ever seen an NBA game. It looked pretty majestic to the eyes of a freshman at Cleveland Benedictine High School.

I was 14 years old in 1969, and my father took me to the game. This was a year before the Cavaliers played their first game, a few months before anyone had a clue Cleveland would have its own NBA team. The Royals played four of their home games at the Cleveland Arena. Ticket prices were $5, $4 and $3. I'm reasonably sure my father bought the $5 seats—although he possibly got some tickets for free from his employer, old Fisher Foods.

I've kept the program for decades because of the autographs.

It's hard to be sure, but it appears Oscar Robertson signed the cover. Inside, there are clear signatures of Willis Reed, Bill Bradley and Dave DeBusschere.

Lots of big names. Those four are also in the Hall of Fame.

There are signatures of three very good pros: Norm Van Lier, Cazzie Russell and Herm Gilliam.

There are also signatures from the not-so-famous: Nate Bowman, Bill Hosket, John Warren and Luther Rackley. A year later, Warren and Rackley would be members of the new Cavaliers.

After the game, many of the players were standing around down by the court. They were in street clothes, waiting for the team bus to come, I guess. All I had to do was take my program down to the court, and the guys signed.

On the back page is one more autograph—my own! I guess I was practicing. Looking at the scrawl of my name, I smiled. Who knew I would go on to sign thousands of books over the years—my books. Or that anyone would ever want my autograph, unless it was on a check to pay a bill.

Staring at the program, I remembered that the Royals had a lead and blew the game at the end. I remembered Bob Cousy being the coach of the Royals. He also was a player. He put himself into the game, messed up an in-bounds pass and his team lost.

But that was all I remembered.

I looked up the details of that game. The Knicks indeed did win, 106-105. The Royals didn't just lose, they collapsed. They gave away a 5-point lead in the last 16 seconds.

Cousy had not played in the NBA in the previous six years. He had been the coach at Boston College, with a 114-38 record. The Royals hired him to take over their team—and also wanted him to play a little bit.

Oscar Robertson fouled out with two minutes left. A 41-year-old Cousy put himself into the game for the first time. He was out of shape, rattled by New York's pressing defense. He made two turn-overs on in-bounds passes. That means he threw away passes on plays that he'd drawn up during timeouts.

That's right, he could not get the ball in-bounds correctly—and the play was his idea!

The NBA coaching life was never kind to Cousy, one of the greatest point guards in NBA history. In five NBA seasons, his record was 141-207 with zero playoff appearances. He then had a good career as a TV broadcaster for the Boston Celtics.

The victory was New York's 18th in a row as they opened that 1969–70 season with a 23-1 record. The Knicks also won the NBA title that year.

Walt Frazier had 27 points in that game, Willis Reed had 19. Oscar Robertson had 33 points, 10 assists and six rebounds. I later learned Robertson and Cousy grew to despise each other that season. A Hall of Famer, Cousy played only 34 minutes in seven games that season, scoring five points.

It was my first NBA game, long before I ever dreamed that I'd be a full-time basketball writer for seven years.

It was long before I would dare to think I'd cover the Cavaliers winning an NBA title. My father and I were simply hoping Cleveland would get pro basketball, maybe the Royals would move north. They played 26 games in Cleveland between 1967 and 1970, according to basketball-reference.com.

When I think of the old Cleveland Arena, I think of men watching games while wearing fedora hats and long coats, my father being one of them.

I think of my father and me eating at a small corned beef place before the game. I can't recall the name or where it was located—other than close to the arena. My father insisted it was the best corned beef in Cleveland.

I think of people smoking while watching games, and no one caring. Smoke hovered above the court, clouds of Lucky Strikes, Camels and Winstons.

I think of how the Royals moved from Cincinnati to Kansas City and finally to Sacramento.

I think of later getting to know Bob Cousy and Willis Reed when I covered the NBA, and how they were very gracious to a young basketball writer.

I think of my father, who loved to take me to games. He's now gone, and so is the Cleveland Arena.

But when I look at that old program, they all remain alive in my memory.

A final note: The attendance was 10,348. That no doubt helped Nick Mileti convince businessmen to invest in his quest to bring Cleveland its own pro basketball team.

CHAPTER 3

Godfather of the Cavs

Understand this about Nick Mileti: He had no money.

To be fair, I'm talking about *money*—as in the world of big league professional sports, where Mileti found a way to bring the National Basketball Association to Cleveland in 1970.

None of what I'm writing is to diminish the accomplishments of Mileti. It was amazing, in its own way. And Mileti was one of the least likely men to pull it off. He wasn't a businessman. He didn't come from wealth. He didn't even seem to have strong political connections.

But he brought big time basketball to Cleveland.

Here's how it began . . .

In 1968, Mileti put together $1.8 million to buy the old Cleveland Arena and the Cleveland Barons of the American Hockey League.

Today, $1.8 million is what a bench-warmer might be paid in the NBA.

But it was a fortune to Mileti, who went to John Adams High on Cleveland's East Side. Public school, tough neighborhood. He graduated in 1949. The Akron Beacon Journal found his high school yearbook. It listed these as Mileti's activities: "Cheerleader, athletic chairman, Distinction Day Committee, Dance Committee, Prom Chairman, Student Council, Corridor Patrol, Merit Roll."

What does that list say about a guy who would eventually own the Indians, Cavaliers, Barons, the Cleveland Arena and the Richfield Coliseum? Oh, he also owned the Cleveland Crusaders of the World Hockey Association. And he owned WWWE radio (now WTAM, 1100-AM).

"Looking back, I don't know how Nick did it," said former Cavaliers broadcaster Joe Tait. "It was almost all Other People's Money."

Perhaps Mileti learned the skill of bringing people together for a common cause. It began all the way back at John Adams High. Let's look at some of the items on his list again:

Athletic chairman.

Prom chairman.

Student council.

Dance committee.

Distinction Day committee.

Cheerleader.

I don't know what some of those activities entailed, other than Mileti putting himself in the middle of where the action was in high school. He wasn't an athlete, but he was a cheerleader and "athletic chairman." He helped organized the prom and activities.

Mileti was brilliant at selling and what some in business call "casting a vision," and then convincing others to follow the verbal picture he painted. In the middle 1960s, he was a lawyer and did some work in the prosecutor's office in the Cleveland suburb of Lakewood. That was his primary job.

According to the first Cleveland Cavaliers media guide in 1970:

> He also did legal work for the group that was seeking a federal loan in order to build the Westerly, an apartment building in Lakewood for senior citizens. Nick established himself quickly as a lawyer who could get things done—even in Washington—and a salesman who could convince a hesitant elderly couple that a move to the Westerly would be a happy decision . . . Nick Mileti became the nation's foremost authority on how to get housing built for elderly people.

That's from the media guide for the team owned by Mileti, so there may have been a touch of hyperbole. But at the heart of it was his ability to sell.

Nick Mileti in 1969 at his Arena. He already owned the Cleveland Barons hockey team, but Mileti had his sights set on an NBA franchise. Now, he just needed money.
Richard J. Misch / The Plain Dealer

He was more than a great salesman. He was a Rembrandt with words. Not only could he make you see his vision, you *felt* it. After a while, you *wanted* it. In fact, *you had to have it!*

As was true in high school, when Mileti became an adult he liked to promote events. On Dec. 14, 1967, he set up a basketball game at the old Cleveland Arena between Bowling Green State University (his alma mater) and Niagara University. He was raising funds for Bowling Green.

My father took me to that game because he was fascinated with Calvin Murphy, Niagara's star. He was listed at 5-foot-9 but seemed smaller. He came to Cleveland as one of the top scorers in college basketball. My father wanted to see him. I was 12 years old and mesmerized by Murphy's quickness, his ability to drive to the rim and score between taller players.

He scored 41 points that night. He fired up 39 shots, made 17. He also was 7-for-9 at the foul line. This was before college had a 3-point shot.

Bowling Green was a 94-86 winner. Bowling Green was coached by a guy named Bill Fitch.

Looking back, two different attendance figures were given for the game: about 8,000 or 11,000. I believe 8,000 was closer to the truth. The arena was pretty full, but not packed.

That game convinced Mileti to find a way to become a player in pro sports—as an owner. Soon, Nick Mileti wasn't just selling a good deal, he was offering you a chance to be a part of his dream . . . with pro sports being the magnet.

He approached investors about putting together cash to bring an NBA team to Cleveland.

A chance to do something special for the city.

A chance to be a part of the pro game.

A chance to have your friends look up to you because you are part of a pro sports ownership group.

Finally, a chance to have fun. There's no business like the sports business!

*   *   *

Nine months after that game, Mileti put together $1.8 million to buy the old Cleveland Arena and the Cleveland Barons of the American Hockey League. About half of that cash came from the Kettering family in Dayton. Mileti had a friend who was a Wall Street banker, and he help put together the deal. He found some other smaller investors, added in some loans . . .

And just like that, Mileti and his investors were in the game.

The Barons were a bit of a distressed property. In the season before Mileti closed the deal, the Barons averaged 4,231 fans—seventh in the eight-team American Hockey League.

Mileti closed the deal for the Arena and the Barons on Sept. 27,

1968. In 1968–69, his first season owning the Barons, attendance dropped to 3,415 per game—eighth in the eight-team league.

But Mileti didn't really want hockey.

He wanted hoops. Pro hoops.

The recently formed American Basketball Association was going after the NBA, looking for cities in which to place franchises. Of course, the ABA was a very iffy proposition from the start. It had the red, white and blue ball. It had the 3-point shot. It also had a lot of owners like Mileti, men with big dreams, few dollars and zero experience in running big time sports franchises.

In the 1968–69 season, the NBA had only 14 franchises. The ABA had 11. Both leagues were willing to expand, trying to beat each other to promising cities. Mileti had looked at joining the National Hockey League, the big leagues. But the NHL wanted $6 million for an expansion free. That was way out of Mileti's price range.

Besides, he wanted basketball, and he wanted the NBA. He believed that would be more attractive to investors in Cleveland.

*   *   *

Which brings us to 1968.

At this point, Mileti was 37 years old. He owned the Cleveland Arena. He owned the Cleveland Barons. He often wore leisure suits, or suits with colorful shirts and wild, wide ties. He had the long sideburns of the late 1960s. By the early 1970s, it was long hair over the ears.

He wanted to look young, hip and prosperous. And he did—at a first glance.

But he still had no money. At least no real money.

No money, no problem!

Mileti had already found a way around that issue to become a minor league hockey owner. Now, he would figure out how to raise money for big league NBA basketball.

The NBA voted to add three more teams for the 1970–71 season.

The entrance fee was to be in the $3.7 million range.

From Mileti's view, he could buy his way into the sport he really wanted—basketball—for half the price of an expansion NHL hockey team.

He just had to find the money.

You can imagine his sales pitch, something like:

"OK, you can't play in the NBA. But how would you like to be a part-owner? You can get great seats. You can meet the players. You will add new friends who want to be around the guy who is an NBA owner."

Close your eyes and think of it . . . you are suddenly a player, even if you're only 5-foot-6 and can't jump over a phone book. (Remember, this was the 1960s when everybody had phone books.)

He found local businessman/banker Bruce Fine, who invested about $300,000 with Mileti.

I knew Fine. I recall him telling me how you could buy into Mileti's early sports ventures for as little as $50,000. Fine wasn't sure if Mileti could make money while owning any of his franchises, but he believed Mileti would eventually sell. And when he did, it would be for a higher price than various investors paid to join the original deal.

That was Mileti's big selling point: Put your money in now—it will be worth a lot more later as the prices of franchises are destined to rise.

As Mileti was talking to the NBA about Cleveland, something else loomed. It was the war between the NBA and the ABA. The NBA rushed its expansion agenda simply to keep the ABA out of some cities. Cleveland was one of those.

On Jan. 20, 1970, the NBA announced it was expanding from 14 to 17 teams. Think about that for a moment. Why add *three* teams? Who wants a league with an odd number of teams? That creates scheduling nightmares.

But the NBA was worried about the ABA going into places such as Cleveland, Buffalo and Portland. So the NBA granted franchises to those cities.

Looking back, it's easy to ask, "Why the rush?"

Cleveland? Buffalo? Portland?

The Cleveland Arena on Euclid Avenue in 1972. This is where it all began for the Cavaliers, but they wouldn't stay long. Visiting players sometimes dressed at the hotel and walked across the street in their uniforms rather than use the Arena's decrepit facilities. *William G. Vorpe / The Plain Dealer*

Portland had zero big league teams in 1970. Buffalo had the Bills and was adding the Sabres in the NHL expansion. Cleveland was the only real "big league city" in 1970, with the Indians and Browns.

But the NBA wanted them all—so they wouldn't go into the ABA. And Mileti couldn't wait to join the hoops party.

*   *   *

Here's how he did it.

I was once an owner of the Cavaliers.

A very small owner.

Mileti had cut a deal with the wealthy Kettering family to own 49% of the Arena and the Barons. The Barons were purchased for $510,000 and the Arena for $1.3 million.

Then, to raise capital for the purchase of the Cavaliers, Mileti sold stock, for $5 a share.

I believe my father bought five shares for $25. What a deal!

In an interview with the Akron Beacon Journal, Mileti said he sold "450,000 shares in a day and a half . . . we raised $2.25 million that way."

The NBA required Mileti to pay $1.5 million up front, then $550,000 in each of the next four seasons.

This deal gets complicated—as did nearly every sports deal involving Mileti. People bought in and later sold out. New investors were recruited.

But the bottom line (at least in 1970) was this: The former high school cheerleader and lawyer was the president of a National Basketball Association team.

In less than three years, he had bought the Arena, the Barons and the new NBA franchise.

From high school cheerleader to pro sports owner.

"It was remarkable," said Joe Tait. "I doubt anything like this can ever happen again because it's a billionaire's game now. But Nick made it happen."

When the team was sold to Gordon Gund in 1983, stock holders were paid off. As for my stock certificates from the Cavs . . . I lost them. But at least my family had an NBA team to watch.

CHAPTER 4

Why Are They Called the Cavaliers?

I remember the 1970 contest to select a nickname for the new Cleveland NBA franchise.

The Plain Dealer asked fans to send suggestions to owner Nick Mileti via the newspaper for a few weeks.

Mileti went through them . . . or at least some of them.

A 2010 Plain Dealer story by Bill Lubinger reported that about 11,000 entries were submitted.

I know I sent in an idea, but I can't remember what nickname I submitted. I used to send in replies to The Plain Dealer in the 1960s and early 1970s. They had "Grandstand Managers" contests in which fans voted on sports issues of the day. Some voters were declared winners and received free Indians tickets.

Former Plain Dealer sports editor Hal Lebovitz was the master of engaging readers, answering questions in his "Ask Hal" column along with his informal polls. In many ways, Lebovitz was doing social media long before computers.

At one point, Lebovitz offered to mail out old sports books and media guides to those who wanted them—first come, first mailed to you. That was when I was in high school and dreaming of having a job like Hal's. I sent a letter asking for whatever he'd be willing to send me. I received a free copy of "Pitchin' Man," the quickie book Lebovitz wrote with Indians pitcher Satchel Paige during the 1948 baseball season. At that point, Lebovitz was a writer with the old Cleveland News.

I write this because people of a certain age tend to think they invented what my business calls "reader engagement" thanks to the Internet.

Guess again.

Naming the Cavaliers via the newspaper was an old-school style of reader engagement.

Lebovitz loved basketball. At 6-foot-3, he was tall for his era, the 1930s, when he played center for Glenville High and what was then called Western Reserve University. He also officiated high school and college basketball games.

He was thrilled with the idea of an NBA team in Cleveland.

And it would be a coup if The Plain Dealer could lead the charge (and engage the readers) by serving as the vehicle to the name the team. The Plain Dealer was then in a newspaper war with the afternoon paper, the Cleveland Press. Convincing Mileti to use The Plain Dealer was a way to keep an edge over the Press.

The contest was a huge hit with readers.

The winner was promised season tickets for the first season.

I doubt Mileti went through all 11,000 entries. I doubt anyone did. But Mileti looked at a lot of them.

He picked this final five:

The Jays. (Jay was his son Jimmy's nickname.)

The Towers.

The Presidents.

The Foresters.

The Cavaliers.

According to Lubinger's story, the names came from these sources:

The Towers came from the Terminal Tower, the tallest building in Cleveland in 1970.

The Presidents because Ohio produced eight presidents of the USA.

The Foresters received a lot of support "because Forest City (stores) had stuffed the ballot box," according to Lubinger.

The Cavaliers was No. 5.

The Cavaliers had a name and a logo. But it took a while for them to add a few wins. Here's their look in 1971. *The Cleveland Press Collection, Michael Schwartz Library, Cleveland State University*

The Plain Dealer came back with another ballot, asking fans to pick from the Final Five. I'm sure I voted.

My guess is I picked The Towers. It seemed to fit a basketball team.

The winning entry came from Jerry Tomko, who lived in Eastlake at the time.

This is part of what The Plain Dealer's Bill Nichols wrote on the day the selection was announced:

> Cavaliers are gallant, courtly soldiers of days gone by. Cavaliers is the name of Cleveland's courtly National Basketball Association team and there is no one happier about the christening than Eastlake's Jerry Tomko.
>
> Tomko won a pair of season tickets for the team's maiden campaign when his letter on why the team should be called

Cavaliers was judged best of more than 11,000 submitted to The Plain Dealer Name The Team Contest.

In part, Tomko's essay read, 'The name Cleveland Cavaliers represents a group of daring fearless men whose life's pact was never surrender, no matter what the odds.'

The winning name was the popular choice of the fans who voted on the five finalists, Cavaliers, Jays, Foresters, Towers and Presidents. More than one-third of the 6,000 votes cast preferred Cavaliers.

In Lubinger's 2010 story, Mileti admitted he didn't know if one-third of the ballots named the Cavaliers.

In the end, he picked Tomko's name "because I liked it."

And that's probably true of most Cavs fans.

CHAPTER 5

Bill Fitch Joins the Team

I first met Bill Fitch in 1985. I was in my first season as a basketball writer with the Akron Beacon Journal, covering the Cavaliers. Fitch was in his 16th season as an NBA head coach. He was with Houston, his third team.

I had admired Fitch from a distance. When I introduced myself to him, he was underwhelmed. I can't recall how the conversation went, but it didn't last long.

Later, I told Cavs broadcaster Joe Tait about it.

"At times, Bill can be a smart ass." Joe told me. "But he's a good guy."

That summed up our first few meetings in those years. Fitch had won a title in Boston (1981). He had made it to the NBA Finals in Houston (1986). He had helped build the Cavaliers. He also was known for imposing his will on others, especially writers covering him. Like many coaches, Fitch was a bit of a control freak.

Things would change dramatically as Fitch grew older and took over the New Jersey Nets and later the L.A. Clippers. Those were two dismal franchises, and he made them respectable. During that time, he mellowed.

We became good friends. My admiration for him grew. He became more patient, more thoughtful, far less driven by ego. That's because he had been knocked down a few times.

Fitch no longer had to live up to the image of his father, who was a Marine. Fitch told me that he prized a picture of himself as child in a Marine uniform, standing next to his father.

He did not have to whip an expansion team into shape, as he had done in Cleveland. He didn't have to prove he was more than some guy from small Coe College who ended up in the NBA.

By 1990, Fitch was more at peace with himself and a much more pleasant man to be around. He probably did some of his best coaching jobs with the Nets and Clippers. In both places, he had a 17-65 record in his first season. And he eventually led them both to the playoffs.

*   *   *

Nick Mileti admitted several times that he knew very little about basketball.

In 1970, he came into the NBA as an owner with zero connections in the pro game. When it came to college basketball, he had a relationship with one and only one coach.

That man was Bill Fitch.

And that explains how Fitch ended up not only as the first coach of the Cavaliers, but also had complete control over every aspect of the basketball operation.

Today, that doesn't seem surprising. Fitch is in the Basketball Hall of Fame as a coach. He was the head coach of the Cavaliers, Celtics, Rockets, Nets and Clippers in a career that spanned 25 seasons.

But on March 18, 1970, Fitch was only 37 years old when he was hired by Mileti and handed the Cleveland expansion franchise.

He never had played or coached a minute in the NBA. He had been a head coach only three seasons at the NCAA Division I level: Bowling Green (1967-68) and the University of Minnesota (1968-70).

Mileti was a Bowling Green graduate. When he promoted a basketball game between Bowling Green and Niagara University at the old Cleveland Arena in 1968, Fitch was coaching his alma mater.

Nick Mileti admitted that he knew little about basketball when he picked the relatively inexperienced Bill Fitch as the Cavs' first coach. Fitch was fine with that—it gave him more control. *The Cleveland Press Collection, Michael Schwartz Library, Cleveland State University*

It's almost impossible to believe anything like this would happen in the modern NBA—a coach with so little experience being trusted with a franchise.

"It was a different NBA back then," Fitch told me.

The league was sort of an afterthought in the pro sports scene, a distant third behind Major League Baseball and the National Football League.

Even the college game was smaller. This was before television and shoe company money poured into the game. In the late 1960s, there were very few college games on national television.

UCLA coach John Wooden was making about $30,000 in 1970. He would retire in 1975 after winning 10 national titles. His final salary was $40,500.

Mileti began courting Fitch even before the NBA approved his application to bring basketball to Cleveland. Fitch was the one coach whom Mileti felt he could trust, due to their Bowling Green connection.

*   *   *

"Bill was very driven and ambitious," said Joe Tait. "I could see that when he was coach at Coe College."

Coe is a small college (about 1,400 students) in Cedar Rapids, Iowa.

Fitch originally was an All-State guard from Davenport, Iowa. He was good enough to be recruited by legendary Kansas coach Phog Allen, but Fitch enlisted in the Marines. His father was a Marine. Turned out, Fitch was underage and soon left the Marines. He enrolled at Coe College, where he played basketball and baseball.

Then he was drafted into the Army. He served two years and was discharged in 1956. He began his coaching career at Creighton, where he was the head baseball coach and assistant basketball coach. Think about this for a moment. Creighton was a major college athletic program. Fitch was coaching two different sports. And he was an assistant in basketball. In baseball, he was the head coach and his star pitcher was future Hall of Famer Bob Gibson.

Then he left Creighton to be the head basketball coach at Coe, his alma mater. These jobs paid so poorly back then, Coe looked better than Creighton to Fitch.

I know this is a lot of history, but it's important to understand what the basketball world was like in the late 1950s when Fitch began his career. He had a 42-40 record as a head coach at Coe.

At that point, Tait was a student/radio broadcaster at Monmouth College in Monmouth, Ill. The two schools were in the same league, and Tait figured out Fitch was a good radio guest. That began a relationship that would eventually pay off big for Tait. But he and Fitch had no clue they'd come together in Cleveland a dozen years later.

Fitch's next stop was the University of North Dakota, where things began to change for Fitch. He took a team that had seven consecutive losing seasons at what is now the Division II level. It took three years, but Fitch began to win and took North Dakota to a pair of NCAA Division II Final Fours, shocking for a school located in Grand Forks.

Fitch used to joke that one way to recruit in North Dakota was to find a good player "who had bad grades in geography," so he wouldn't know how far away and how cold it was compared to most basketball hotbeds.

His star was Phil Jackson, who later played in the NBA and became a Hall of Fame coach with Chicago and the L.A. Lakers.

"I got to know NBA people like (Boston Celtics coach) Red Auerbach when I was coaching Phil," said Fitch.

It also was when he first began to think the NBA could be a destination for him.

His next step was Bowling Green, where he had an 18-7 record in 1967-68—and where he met Mileti, an alumnus and supporter of the school. His team was picked to finish last in the Mid-American Conference, but won it with a 10-2 conference record. He led them to an NCAA tournament bid. His Bowling Green team lost 72-71 to Marquette and future Hall of Fame coach Al McGuire in the first round.

That was enough for the University of Minnesota to hire Fitch. At the age of 36, he was a head coach in the Big Ten.

Once again, he took over a team picked last in its conference—and had success. His record at Minnesota was 12-12 and 13-11 in two seasons.

Mileti followed his career.

His list of possible coaches for the Cavaliers contained only one name—Bill Fitch.

*   *   *

Fitch was making about $20,000 a year to coach Minnesota. This was 1970, so that was very respectable money for the time. It also was an era when big time college coaches didn't make more money than school presidents. Or the governor of the state. They weren't the highest paid public employees in their states, as is often the case today, including football coaches at Ohio State and Alabama.

In a March 19, 1970, interview with Sid Hartman of the Minneapolis Tribune, Fitch explained why he went to the Cavaliers:

> The offer was just so fabulous I couldn't turn it down. The salary is a lot more than I'm making at Minnesota, plus I have a big stock option. I've signed a three-year contract and, in addition to being coach, I will be director of player personnel, which puts me in complete authority in all player matters.
>
> Nick Mileti has been a close friend of mine since I coached at Bowling Green . . . I have to think of my family and their future. With Cleveland I probably will make as much in three years as I would make in 10 years at Minnesota.

Hartman estimated Fitch's salary with the Cavs at $60,000 annually.

Hartman also quoted Fitch as saying: "I've been coaching for 20 years and I still don't own my house."

*   *   *

Fitch knew what Mileti didn't know. That is, he knew Mileti had no clue about the NBA and wasn't likely to try to influence the coach's decisions.

And Fitch knew Mileti was desperate. If the only way Mileti could convince Fitch to take the job was to give Fitch total control of the basketball end of the franchise, well, Fitch received total control.

To help him, Fitch hired Jim Lessig as "assistant coach and chief scout." This was when NBA teams had only one assistant coach and chief scout. But Fitch didn't pick someone with NBA experience

Bill Fitch runs a rookie practice. In those days, NBA teams had only one assistant coach. *The Cleveland Press Collection, Michael Schwartz Library, Cleveland State University*

to help him. Instead, Lessig was his assistant coach and freshman basketball coach at Minnesota.

I've spent a lot of time on how Fitch was hired because I've long wondered about it. Not in 1970, when I was 15 years old. But about 15 years later when I was on the NBA basketball beat for the Akron Beacon Journal.

I know, Cleveland has a strange history with coaches. In 1980, Cavs owner Ted Stepien turned the basketball operations over to another coach from Minnesota—Bill Musselman. But I dismiss nearly every basketball decision made by Stepien because when it came to basketball, Stepien was easily influenced, ill-prepared and overwhelmed as an NBA owner.

Bill Fitch recently said I was underestimating him back then. His point was that I was viewing the then-38-year-old Fitch through modern basketball eyes, not the reality of the NBA in 1970. The league was a bit of the Wild West, where coaches could recreate themselves.

"What about Dick Motta and Cotton Fitzsimmons?" Fitch asked me.

In 1968, Motta went from coaching at Weber State to head coach of the Chicago Bulls.

In 1970, Cotton Fitzsimmons went from coaching at Kansas State to head coach of the Phoenix Suns. Before that, Fitzsimmons was a junior college coach.

"How much more NBA experience did they have?" asked Fitch. It's a good point.

Motta coached for 25 years in the NBA, Fitzsimmons for 21.

And the 1970–71 season was the start of a 25-year NBA coaching career for Fitch.

CHAPTER 6

Basketball Cards and Bubblegum

Bill Fitch was hired as the head coach of the Cleveland Cavaliers on March 19, 1970.

Four days later, Fitch was in charge of the Cavs' college draft.

Talk about setting up the three expansion teams—Cleveland, Buffalo and Portland—for failure. These teams weren't admitted into the NBA until Feb. 6, 1970. They had to find coaches, scouts and front office people.

And prepare for the draft, looming six weeks away. It took Cavs owner Nick Mileti five weeks to convince Fitch to leave the University of Minnesota for the NBA.

Four days later, it was college draft time.

While writing this book, I've become fascinated by how the Cavs were born. The answer is, "Outrageously premature."

I know Fitch had a copy of Street & Smith's Magazine. That was the bible of college basketball in the era. It contained information on players, coaches and college teams.

This was before the Internet. This was when it was very hard to even receive accurate statistics from some schools. It was when NBA coaches tried to stand close to college players to determine if the listed size of the players was correct. Often, it was more like wishful thinking.

Before taking the Cavaliers job, Fitch coached in the Big Ten for two seasons. What players did he know best?

Those who played in the Big Ten.

This was the era of the NBA having 19 rounds. Teams seemed to keep drafting until they ran out of names. By the 19th round, only three teams were still selecting players.

The Cavs selected four Big Ten players in the first six rounds of the draft:

1. John Johnson, Iowa.
2. Dave Sorenson, Ohio State.
3. Surry Oliver, Stephen F. Austin.
4. Glen Vidnovic, Iowa.
5. Wayne Sokolowski, Ashland.
6. Joe Cooke, Indiana.

Stephen F. Austin and Ashland were in the "small college" level of NCAA basketball back then. The other four players were from Big Ten schools.

"I really thought JJ (Johnson) was a good player," said Fitch. "And I was right. He had a very good NBA career."

The 6-foot-7 Johnson was a big time college player, averaging 28 points per game as a senior at Iowa. He also shot 57 percent.

Johnson played 12 years in the NBA. Only the first three were with the Cavs, where he averaged 16 points and 7.1 rebounds. He died in 2016 at the age of 68.

In the second round, Fitch drafted Dave Sorenson, a 6-foot-8 forward from Ohio State. I remember being very excited about that pick because Sorenson and the Buckeyes had several of their games carried on Cleveland television. He was a college star, a 24-point scorer who averaged 9.0 rebounds and shot 55 percent from the field.

Sorenson played only 213 NBA games over three seasons. He averaged 8.1 points per game in his career. His best season was as a rookie, when he averaged 11.3 points for the expansion Cavs. Sorenson died in 2002 at the age of 54.

The only other player in that first Cavs draft to even play in the NBA was sixth-rounder Joe Cooke. The 6-foot-3 guard from Indiana appeared in 73 games that season for the Cavs. It was his only year in the NBA. He died in 2006 at the age of 58.

When Bill Fitch was hired as head coach of the Cavaliers on March 19, 1970, he had just weeks to prepare for the college draft. His research materials? A copy of Street & Smith's Magazine ... and basketball trading cards.
Author's collection

It's impossible to criticize or even critique this first draft. Fitch was placed in a daunting position. The NBA didn't allow the three expansion teams to have high picks.

Too bad.

The first four selections in the 1970 draft became Hall of Famers: Bob Lanier (Pistons), Rudy Tomjanovich (Rockets), Pete Maravich (Hawks) and Dave Cowens (Celtics).

The expansion teams were assigned slots 7-8-9, with the Cavs picking seventh. The rest of the first round featured only one player with a higher NBA scoring average as a rookie than Johnson's 16.6 points—Geoff Petrie (Portland, 24.8).

The college draft was a yawner, a list of names in small agate type in most newspapers around the country.

Johnson was just leaving his literature class at Iowa when he learned he was picked by the Cavs. He averaged 16.6 points, 6.8 rebounds and 4.8 assists as a rookie.

"JJ was just a very good all-around player," said Joe Tait.

The "point forward" phrase would come into the NBA vocabulary several years later. The point forward was a forward who could handle the ball, pass and set up his teammates. That was Johnson from the moment he stepped on the floor in the NBA.

He played only three years with the Cavs, then was part of a huge trade with Portland. The Cavs acquired the No. 2 pick in the 1973 draft and used it on Minnesota power forward Jim Brewer. He turned out to be a solid rebounder and defender, but Johnson was a superior player.

An interesting side story to that deal came from something I found in the New York Times when Brewer passed up a chance to sign with the rival ABA and instead went with Cleveland: "Brewer said the reason he signed with Cleveland was because of Bill Fitch, who recruited Brewer when Fitch coached at Minnesota."

*   *   *

The story is true.

For years, Fitch told the media and friends how he used basketball trading cards to do homework on the 1970 NBA expansion draft.

Each NBA team was allowed to protect seven players, meaning three expansion teams (Cleveland, Buffalo and Portland) were picking the eighth best player on each team . . . at least in theory. No established team could lose more than three players.

This was decades before the Internet.

"I gave Jim Lessig 20 bucks and told him to buy all the basketball cards he could find," said Fitch. "They had stats and other basic information on the back."

I used to buy basketball cards. The information on the back was *very* basic—height, weight, age, college and rudimentary stats like free throws and rebounds.

Fitch and Lessig also collected a lot of bubblegum. These were the days of five cards in a pack, and a pack was a nickel—with a pink stick of sugary bubblegum.

Hey, they had to start somewhere. This was only six weeks after Fitch was hired as Cleveland's coach. Fitch and the new Cavs had zero NBA background. The same with Lessig, his assistant from college. And the front office was so small, there were no other "basketball people" in place to help.

Furthermore, the three expansion teams were told they had only 48 hours to study the list of players available before the draft began. Lessig's son collected basketball cards, and that gave Lessig and Fitch the idea of buying cards—and then spreading them out on a table.

There were only 99 cards of different NBA players printed by the Topps Company for the 1969–1970 season. Some players available in the expansion draft didn't have their own cards.

This was the era when you wanted to start a franchise with a big guy. It was a center-dominated league. The Sunday afternoon national NBA television broadcast on ABC often featured Bill Russell vs. Wilt Chamberlain.

They were the two biggest of the NBA big men in terms of talent.

The first pick in the 1970 college draft was Bob Lanier, a wide, 6-foot-10 center from St. Bonaventure who was selected by Detroit.

The NBA didn't have the 3-point shot in 1970. Offenses were often set up to throw passes to the center near the rim. The shorter the shot, the better, in the eyes of most coaches.

The Cavs' first pick in the expansion draft was Walt Wesley.

The back of his basketball card would reveal he was 6-foot-10, 220 pounds and 25 years old. It would have these stats from his 1969–70 season with the Chicago Bulls:

72 games played.

270 field goals made.

145 free throws made.

455 rebounds.

655 points scored.

9.5 scoring average.

There were no shooting percentages from the field or foul line. There were no rebounding averages per game.

How do I know what was on the back of Wesley's basketball card? I Googled "Walt Wesley basketball card, 1970." It popped up. A few different clicks, and I found pictures of the front and back of the card.

And I was alarmed at how little information was available to Fitch as he approached the expansion draft.

Another click, and I was on the www.basketball-reference.com website. From there, I learned Wesley not only averaged 9.5 points, but also 6.3 rebounds in 19.5 minutes a game for the Chicago Bulls.

Why did the Bulls expose Wesley to the expansion draft?

A look the 1969–70 Chicago Bulls stats shows the team had 6-foot-10 Tom Boerwinkle as its starting center. Wesley was a backup on a team that also had All-Star forward Chet Walker and Bob Love.

In three minutes and a couple of Internet searches, I probably knew more about Wesley than Fitch did on the day the Cavs drafted him.

Fitch continued his quest for big men by drafting Luther Rackley, a 24-year-old backup center from the Cincinnati Royals.

I'm not going to deal with most of the expansion picks. They did select five-time All-Star Don Ohl, who decided to retire rather than report to the Cavs. In 1970, Ohl was 34 years old. He had averaged only 6.2 points in the 1969–70 season with Atlanta. After 11 years in the NBA, Ohl was not ready for No. 12 with what most basketball people believed would be one of the worst teams in NBA history. So he quit.

I actually followed the expansion draft, very curious what players they'd pick. And I had basketball cards.

I was very excited when they picked Johnny Egan, one of the NBA's shortest players at 5-foot-11. He played in the same Providence College backcourt with Lenny Wilkens. He was a point guard with the Los Angeles Lakers when they played in the NBA Finals in 1969 and 1970. I actually saw him on TV in some of those games.

Egan was 31 years old when the Cavs drafted him. He was never a star, but a solid NBA starter and later in his career, a reliable substitute. He was an old-fashioned, pass-first point guard. He set up the offense, didn't make careless turnovers and could connect on an open outside shot.

But at this stage of his career, he didn't want to spend his 10th pro season with a dismal expansion team. Almost from the moment he was selected by the Cavs, he begged them to trade him. He played 26 games in Cleveland, then Fitch shipped Egan to the San Diego Rockets for a third-round pick in 1971. Egan played two seasons for that franchise, and later became its head coach for 3½ seasons when the team moved to Houston.

The Cavs' most interesting selection was Bobby "Bingo" Smith. He was the No. 6 overall pick in the 1969 draft. A year later, the San Diego Rockets refused to put him on their protection list. He averaged a respectable 7.3 points as a rookie, playing only 16 minutes a game. He was the ideal expansion draft pick, only 24 years old and a former first-rounder who was likely to improve.

And after Smith played 10 years with the Cavs, you can say that Fitch and his basketball card scouting system found a player whose No. 7 uniform was retired by the Cavs.

"You look back at how the franchise was born, and it came from basketball cards and bubblegum," said Joe Tait.

CHAPTER 7

Small Town Guy with a Big League Voice

The voice.

That's how Bill Fitch begins to tell the story of how Joe Tait came to the Cleveland Cavaliers.

It's the voice Fitch first heard when he was a coach at little Coe College in Cedar Rapids, Iowa. While he was the basketball coach at the Iowa school, he also scouted games of opposing teams for Coe's football team.

And Tait?

He was the broadcaster of the Monmouth College (Ill.) football and basketball teams. Fitch would be in the press box scouting a Coe-Monmouth football game.

Remember, this was 1950s small college football when a press box was really a box.

"You could hear Joe everywhere," said Fitch.

Tait got to know Fitch because everyone got to know everyone in the matchbox of a press box.

"He was so well-prepared," said Fitch. "And that voice . . . "

Tait would interview Fitch at halftime of the football games between Coe and Monmouth.

"I'd ask a question and let him talk," said Tait. "He made it easy."

Monmouth had awful football teams during this era.

"But Joe made them sound so good," said Fitch. "His team would

Joe Tait was bouncing around from one small radio station to another. Then Bill Fitch called. Fitch said he knew Tait had the voice to "become something special." *Courtesy of Joe Tait*

be behind 66-0 and he'd make it sound like the score was 6-6."

Tait was 20 years old.

How did he end up in radio? He had an idea and approached radio station WRAM, "The Pride of Beef Country." He talked them into giving him a 15-minute sports show—and the Monmouth College football games.

Why did they let a college kid do that?

He would not be paid.

He had to sell commercial time on the broadcasts. If he sold enough commercials to buy the time, he could go on the air.

You guessed it. He sold enough commercials.

The only money he was paid by the radio station was to be the janitor—10 bucks a week.

Remember this saying: "Little fish sometimes grow up to be big fish." That's a business principle. It means those who are mature in their jobs would be wise to be kind to the "younger people" in their profession. Odds are, at least a few of them will grow to be a big fish—maybe even your boss.

Once in a while, two little fish become friends and surface in the great lakes of media and sports at almost the same time.

That was Tait & Fitch.

Fitch was only 23 years old when he met Tait.

The connection would later be life-changing for Tait. Bill Fitch is the reason Tait had the chance to become one of the greatest broadcasters in Cleveland history.

Even at that young age, Fitch knew Tait had the voice to "become something special."

"I didn't know Bill would become a great coach," said Tait. "But the first time I interviewed him, I knew he'd be a great guest."

When Tait saw Fitch coach his Coe basketball teams, he said, "You could just tell. Bill was not going to spend the rest of his life coaching at places like Coe. He was going somewhere."

As Fitch climbed the college coaching ladder, Tait went from small town station to small town station in Indiana and Illinois:

Decatur, Illinois, where he was "Jolly Joe Tait," the morning voice of WDZ.

Rockford, Illinois, where he was "The Morning Mayor." In fact, Tait said, he "did two terms as morning mayor in Rockford. I had the job twice."

Frankfort, Indiana, where the station prided itself on being "Home of the Hot Dogs." That was the nickname of the local high school team.

The Twin Cities. Not Minneapolis and St. Paul—it was WJBC in Bloomington/Normal, Illinois.

Terre Haute, Indiana, where he once did the radio play-by-play of an arm-wrestling match.

Tait also spent three years teaching broadcasting at Ohio University in Athens. He also broadcast some of the school's sports events.

"Bill was coaching at Bowling Green (1967–68) when I was at Ohio U.," said Tait. "We touched base. They had a preseason media poll of what team would win the Mid-American Conference basketball title. Bowling Green got only one vote for first place."

Tait said a media friend from Toledo was the person who told Fitch about his team's single first-place vote.

"I bet that came from that dumbass Tait down at Ohio U.," said Fitch.

That was the 1967–68 season.

Guess what?

Bowling Green finished with a 10-2 MAC record and won the conference. After a single season, Fitch was off to Minnesota and the Big Ten. The next season, Minnesota played Ohio U., and Tait interviewed Fitch about his new job in the Big Ten.

In 1969, Tait returned to Indiana radio where he did pregame shows for the Indiana Pacers of the old American Basketball Association. He also did some Indiana University football games.

He applied for several major market broadcasting jobs, including positions at WLW in Cincinnati, KMOX in St. Louis and WLS in Chicago.

Lots of rejections. Tait still has the rejection letters.

In 1970, Tait was back in Terre Haute as the Morning Mayor.

He was 33 years old. He had worked his way up from the bottom of the radio barrel to a point where he could see the top, but doubted he'd ever reach it.

He saw a story in the Terre Haute newspaper about Fitch being named head coach of the Cavaliers. Tait sent him this note:

"I always knew you'd make it in the big time. By the way, if you ever need anyone to do for the Cleveland Cavaliers what I did for those Monmouth Fighting Scots (66-0), let me know. Ha! Ha! Ha!"

Tait said he mailed the letter and forgot about it.

"I didn't have any idea it would lead to anything."

At one point, Tait thought he had the job as a play-by-play man for the Montreal Expos. The Expos liked his audition tape, but wanted an announcer from Canada.

"I even applied for a job to do the Saskatchewan Roughriders in the Canadian Football League," said Tait. "They offered, but it was at least a third less than what I was making in Bloomington, Illinois."

By this point, in the fall of 1970, Tait was very discouraged.

*   *   *

The Cavaliers opened their first season with a seven-game trip. Check out this journey:

Buffalo
Portland
San Francisco
Portland
San Diego
Phoenix
Los Angeles

Seven games in 11 days, including two trips to Portland. They lost all seven games, the average margin of defeat being 17 points.

Welcome to expansion basketball. A miserable schedule with a roster that was set up to lose—and lose big.

"In the middle of that trip, I got a call from Fitch," said Tait. "He said Bob Brown was doing the games on the radio. Bob was Nick Mileti's top assistant. Nick didn't want Bob flying all over the country. He needed Bob in Cleveland."

Tait was stunned by the call and said little at first.

"We're getting our brains beat out," said Fitch. "We have to find someone else to do the radio. If you want to come to Cleveland, we'll set you up for the home opener. Tape record the game. We'll give it to Mileti. If he likes it and based on my recommendation, you'll get the job."

Tait jumped at the chance. He was given a room at the old Midtown Sheraton Hotel, right across the street from the old Cleveland Arena. He sat in the hockey press box, high off the court behind one of the baskets and did the game into a tape recorder.

It was opening night for the Cavs' new franchise in Cleveland. Mileti had the idea of giving miniature wine glasses with a Cavs logo on them to all the fans.

Joe Tait recorded his Cavaliers audition tape in the hockey press box at the old Arena, high above the action. Later he would call games from a court-side seat, as shown here at the Coliseum. *Courtesy of Joe Tait*

"His idea was to have everyone get a glass, pass out the wine and then toast the team," said Tait. "But the problem was they couldn't get a liquor license from the state of Ohio. They toasted the team with empty wine glasses . . . Here was a team that had lost all its games, playing in a half-empty arena for a home opener and fans standing there with empty wine glasses."

At the end of the first quarter, San Diego had a 38-17 lead. It was 59-45 at halftime. The attendance for that Oct. 28, 1970, game was announced at 6,144. That probably was optimistic. The Cavs lost, 110-99. Elvin Hayes scored 40 points for the San Diego Rockets.

"After the game, Bob Brown came and took the tape," said Tait. "He said he'd give the tape to Mileti. They'd listen to it that night and call in the morning."

At 9 a.m., Tait's hotel phone rang. He was to come to the arena for a meeting with Mileti.

He walked into the office.

"I like your work," said Mileti. "Bill Fitch says you're perfect for this job, so it's yours."

Tait was hired for $100 a game.

"There were 74 games left, so that added up to $7,400," said Tait. "I was making $10,000 in Indiana."

Tait had spent 10 years chasing the dream of doing big league radio sports. He bounced from one small station to another, working at some of them twice. He made no real money. At the age of 33, he didn't seem to have much future in radio.

Then Bill Fitch called.

Then Nick Mileti made him an offer he could have refused—but in his heart, he knew he couldn't.

Mileti put out his hand.

Tait took it.

Deal.

Tait did two more home games . . .

A 125-110 loss to Cincinnati in front of 3,199 fans.

A 131-107 loss to Atlanta in front of 3,533 fans.

Tait drove home to Indiana to pack up his family and move to Cleveland. The 0-10 Cavs hit the road for Philadelphia.

"I listened to the Cavs game on a Philadelphia radio station— WCAU," said Tait. "The Cavs lost 141-87. The broadcasters were saying things like this was the worst team they'd ever seen and why would anyone want to watch this atrocity? Sonny Hill (analyst) even wondered out loud if the Cavs would survive the season."

Tait said his first wife Edith was listening to the game with him.

"As she packed, she was slam dunking socks into the suitcase and she was really upset," said Tait. "I was wondering, 'What have I done?' But when I told my old station I was leaving, they said the station had just been sold and everyone was being fired."

So Tait was able to tell his wife, "If we stay here, we have no job. At least we have a job in Cleveland."

I talked to Tait about this 49 years after he came to Cleveland. He still had the scorecard he drew on a yellow legal pad for that first game audition tape.

So many things fell into place for Tait.

Fitch claims he can't remember any note from Tait congratulating him about getting the Cavs job. He remembers talking to Mileti and Brown about the kind of broadcaster the team needed.

It had to be someone relatively young who'd work cheap and be absolutely thrilled to do the games of what was likely to be one of the worst teams in NBA history.

"I have just the guy," said Fitch. "Joe Tait."

Brown and Mileti had never heard of Tait. But at this point, they were open to suggestions. They needed someone quick and someone who was almost ready to work for free.

That was Tait, the right guy at the right time.

"And I still have that empty wine glass from opening night," Tait said.

CHAPTER 8

The Awful, Wonderful, Frightful First Year

Now, the stories from the Cleveland Cavaliers' first season are funny and quaint. That's because we know the Cavaliers survived the 1970–71 season. We know Bill Fitch went on to become a Hall of Fame coach. We know Joe Tait became a Hall of Fame radio broadcaster.

We even know Bobby "Bingo" Smith went from being picked in the 1970 expansion draft by the Cavs to having his No. 7 retired by the franchise.

We may even know the story of the San Francisco security guard and Bill Fitch. The Cavs had an 0-14 record. They were playing on the road against the Warriors. Cavs assistant coach Jim Lessig, Tait and Fitch walked into the arena. A security guard asked to see their credentials.

Lessig and Tait had the proper passes.

Fitch did not.

"I left it back at the hotel," said Fitch, explaining he was the coach of the team.

"I've got to see a pass," said the security guard.

"I don't have it," said Fitch,

"How do I know you're the coach of the team?" asked the security guard.

"Do you know the Cavs' record?" asked Fitch.

"It's 0-and-14," said the guard.

"Why would I say I was the coach of the Cavaliers unless I was the coach of the Cavaliers?" asked Fitch.

"Go right in," said the guard.

Fitch did, and wished the guard had sent him back to the hotel room.

The Warriors walloped the Cavs, 109-74.

"The game wasn't even that close when you watched it," said Tait, who told me the Fitch/security guard story.

Yes, it's funny in the rearview mirror of life.

But not when he was a 38-year-old NBA rookie coach.

"I was 0-and-15," he said. "I had never lost 15 games in any season I coached in college."

Tait said logic indicated in an 82-game season, at some point you were destined to win at least *some* games. But opening the season with a 15-game losing streak made Fitch and some of the players wonder, "Will we ever win a game?"

Many years ago, I remember a veteran sportswriter talking about a team on a long losing streak.

"You know, nowhere is it written that they must win another game," he said.

That's true.

Fitch had a lot of one-liners for the media designed to take the attention off the team.

"War is bad," he said. "Expansion is worse."

Fitch's father was a Marine. Fitch also was in the military. He knew war was war and basketball is a game.

But he also knew there was a certain emotional death that comes from losing night after night . . .

After night . . .

After night . . .

Fitch came into the NBA knowing expansion would be hard, but not realizing how the odds were stacked against all three expansion teams—Buffalo, Portland and Cleveland. They were not allowed to pick at the top of the college draft. Their selections were 7-8-9 in the first round.

The expansion draft produced primarily players rejected by established teams—too young, too old, too injured, too slow, too small . . . too something.

By the time they lost that 15th game in a row in San Francisco, the Cavs had played only five home games. That loss to the Warriors was the start of a five-game trip with the first four on the West Coast and the fifth in Baltimore!

"The name is Fitch, not Houdini," was one of his lines when asked about how it felt to keep losing in an expansion situation.

The comment drew some smiles, at least from those who recalled Houdini was a magical escape artist.

But Fitch was trapped in the deep pit of NBA expansion basketball without a ladder. It was a dark, lonely place for a young coach.

Later in his career, Fitch admitted there were nights he could not sleep. There were times when he was sure he'd burst into tears as he stared at the ceiling, wishing sleep would come.

"We won our first game in Portland," said Tait. "It was the Skull Game."

Tait was with Fitch. They had dined at a Portland Chinese restaurant called The Mustang. Food was plentiful, prices were cheap in an era when NBA meal money was $20 a day on the road.

"We left the restaurant and were walking around town," said Tait. "We passed a magic shop. Fitch saw a skull in the window. He went in and bought it for $1.95."

The next night, Fitch talked to the team before the game in Portland. The Cavs had tied Denver's record for opening the season at 0-15.

Fitch held up the skull and said, "This is all that's left of the Denver coach."

He then had all the players touch the skull before they went to play the Blazers.

That night, the Cavs beat Portland, 105-103.

That made the Cavs' record 1-15.

Portland dropped to 5-11. The Blazers had played only three road games.

The Cavaliers' media guide for "Year 1" was a budget affair and a two-fer, sharing a binding with the Cleveland Barons' program. *Author's collection*

Even the schedule was stacked against the expansion Cavaliers. The night after that first win in Portland, the Cavs played in Seattle. Once again, the players touched the skull. They lost by 20 points in Seattle.

*   *   *

In 16 years as a college coach, Fitch's longest losing streak was four games.

"Two years ago, I was the (college) coach of the year in Ohio and the state legislature passed a resolution praising my achievements," Fitch told Sports Illustrated. "This year, they'll probably pass a law against me."

After that victory in Portland, the Cavs put together another losing streak—12 in a row.

At one point, Fitch joked, "Hope springs eternal. We could be the only team in the league that has had all its flu shots."

But when a team starts the season at 1-27, the jokes don't sound very funny.

*   *   *

On Dec. 9, 1970, the Cavs had a home game against Portland. They carried a 2-27 record on the court, and they were behind by three points at the end of the third quarter.

To start the fourth quarter, Cleveland center Walt Wesley won the jump ball. He tipped the ball to teammate Bobby Lewis. The veteran guard (still begging the team to trade him) threw a pass to teammate John Warren.

Things were looking good—a possible fast break layup. Warren caught the ball and headed for the rim—being chased down by Portland's LeRoy Ellis. Warren made the layup, Ellis failing to block the shot.

One problem.

The ball went into the wrong basket.

Two points for . . . Portland!

Even when the Cavs scored, it counted for the other team—or so it seemed.

After the game, Fitch told the media, "The way we've been playing, I'm surprised Warren made that shot."

The wrong-way basket is a famous early Cavs story.

But late in the fourth quarter of that same game, Tait noticed Portland had six players on the court—one too many.

Tait was screaming on the radio broadcast: "PORTLAND HAS SIX GUYS OUT THERE." He sat at the press table near the Cavs bench.

Fitch heard Tait, counted the Portland players, then yelled at the officials: "Portland has six guys out there!"

The officials then counted, and six was indeed the number. Portland was hit with a technical foul.

Didn't matter.

Nick Mileti and NBA commissioner Walter Kennedy celebrate the Cavaliers' first home opener. Mileti's idea was to give all attendees a glass of wine and toast the team. But without the proper liquor license, the glasses wound up empty. *The Cleveland Press Collection, Michael Schwartz Library, Cleveland State University*

Cavs lost, 109-102.

The announced attendance at the Cleveland Arena was 2,002.

*   *   *

It's easy now to make fun of the first-year Cavaliers. They were awful.

There was Gary Suiter, a strange guy who played at Midwestern University in Wichita Falls, Texas. The 6-foot-9 forward made the team as an undrafted free agent.

He played little early in the season. The Cavs were receiving phone calls from someone saying Suiter should play more. Eventually, the Cavs figured out Suiter was making the calls.

The Cavs media guide reads: "No one on the Cavs squad has a greater desire than Suiter to make it as pro."

Well . . . maybe not quite true.

The Cavs also caught Suiter going through some luggage belonging to teammate Larry Mikan. That was a bit creepy, or maybe he was just looking for something to steal.

Suiter finally was cut when Cavs trainer Ron Culp found Suiter in line at an arena hot dog stand—in his Cavs uniform—about an hour before the game.

After he was released, Suiter went down the street to a funeral parlor. He told the director he was a member of the Cavaliers, had lost a parent and needed to make funeral arrangements. Could he use the phone to call some family members?

He was calling other teams, asking for tryouts.

A month after Suiter was cut, someone from the funeral home came by with a $750 phone bill—for calls made by Suiter.

His NBA career lasted 30 games and 140 minutes. In 1982, Suiter was murdered over a $275 gambling debt.

*   *   *

The Cavs briefly had a forward named McCoy McLemore. He was picked in the 1970 expansion draft. He was a starter for the Cavs, averaging 11.7 points and 8.0 rebounds.

But the seven-year veteran wanted to go to a good team. He was traded late in that first season to Milwaukee, where he was a backup on the 1971 Bucks team that won the NBA title.

I later met McLemore when I was a volunteer with Bill Glass Prison Ministries. McLemore would speak at some of the weekend prison events. One of his talks was about answered prayers: how God answered his prayer to get him out of Cleveland. He went from the NBA's worst team to the best.

He told me it was nothing against the city of Cleveland.

"The team was so bad and it was really a tough situation for a veteran player," he said. "A lot of the older guys felt that way."

McLemore later worked as a broadcaster for the Houston Rockets, along with his ministry activities. He died in 2009 of cancer at the age of 67.

I remember one of his talks where he said he "went from playing next to (center) Luther Rackley in Cleveland to Kareem Abdul-Jabbar (in Milwaukee). Talk about how something good came from something bad!"

*   *   *

Most of the guys were sincere. They worked hard. They cared about winning and losing.

And they were worried.

Soon, it became obvious the Nick Mileti ownership group was having financial problems. The front office staff was small.

When the calendar turned to 1971, the Cavs had a 5-39 record. Only two home crowds were over 4,000.

Tait was calling the games on radio station WERE, 1300-AM. It had a very weak signal.

A few years later, the Cavs were on 1100-AM, a 50,000-watt powerhouse. Legendary sports talk show host Pete Franklin used to tell listeners he could be heard in "38 states and half of Canada!"

He was once asked about WERE.

"It reaches 38 streets and half of the West Side of Cleveland!" said Franklin.

That wasn't too far from the truth, especially at night when the radio signal seemed even more feeble.

"I swear, at night you couldn't hear us at the Greyhound station, and that was only a mile away from the arena," said Tait.

Tait insisted he received only five fan letters during the entire first season.

"I got 10 the year I was Morning Mayor of Monmouth," said Tait.

For a while during the season, Tait lived out of the Midtown Sheraton across the street from the arena. He first roomed with Larry Mikan, then with Joe Cooke.

That's right, to save money, the radio broadcaster was sharing a small hotel room with players.

He eventually moved to Parma Heights when his family joined him.

* * *

The Arena on Euclid Avenue and East 37th Street was in a very rough neighborhood.

"We used to lead the league in stolen cars," said Fitch.

It was a line that drew laughs. But one night after a game, Fitch was walking out of the arena. A man was talking into a pay-phone. He was explaining to someone how his car had been stolen.

He was crying.

This was no joke.

My father took me to some games during the first year. We used to buy tickets for two bucks from scalpers selling them in front of the arena—below cost at the ticket window.

My father spent extra money to park his car near the Arena in a lot with a fence, a gate and a private security guard.

"The opposing teams used to call the arena the 'Black Hole of Calcutta,' " said Tait. "The visiting teams stayed at the hotel across the street. They walked across in their uniforms. They were afraid to shower at the Arena."

Tait told a story of arriving a little later than normal for a game because of a snow storm.

"As I drove past the Arena, there was Wilt Chamberlain in his purple and gold uniform," said Tait. "He was in the middle of the street heading to the arena, and I almost hit him."

Fitch did fix up the Cavs locker room and made sure the water was in working order.

"I didn't care about the visitors," he said. "(Boston star) John Havlicek said he was sure he'd catch a contagious disease if he showered there. That's why he dressed at the Midtown Hotel across the street."

Austin Carr was shocked by the Arena when he joined the Cavs in the fall of 1971 after playing at Notre Dame.

"The floor was so bad, you would bounce the ball in certain spots and nails would pop out of the court," he said. "One nail bounced up and hit me in the chin!"

Carr said the floor "had dead spots. You'd dribble and the ball would just die, barely bounce back up."

He had some friends who discovered a way to climb onto the Arena roof. They found a hole and then would slip into the game and watch it for free.

Fitch said he'd take a pistol behind the Arena and shoot huge rats that were running around near the garbage cans.

"I got the gun because I took it off a guy after a game," said Fitch.

"I know that's true," said Carr. "On days we practiced, they had some big garbage cans near the floor. They had some cats to eat the rats. We'd hear them fighting when we were practicing."

Funny stuff . . . now.

"It was cold in there a lot," said Carr. "The hockey team (Cleveland Barons) played there and you sometimes could feel the ice under the court."

Old, cold and dangerous.

That was the home of the Cavaliers.

No wonder McLemore was praying to be traded.

*　　　*　　　*

Tait kept hearing rumors the team could possibly fold after the first season.

According to its first media guide, the team had only eight people working for them. Four of them also worked for the minor league Barons, also owned by Mileti.

That media guide sold for a dollar. But you got two teams for the price of one. Half of the media guide covered the Barons, half was the Cavs. It was 52 pages.

The Cavs ended up with a 15-67 record, the worst in the NBA that season.

"We were 2-10 against Portland and 7-5 against Buffalo," said Tait, who remembered those stats nearly 50 years after that season.

That meant the Cavs were 9-15 vs. fellow expansion teams and 6-52 against the rest of the NBA.

"We were like the Mayo Clinic for the NBA," said Fitch. "Other teams came to us to be healed."

Tait said he once saw Bingo Smith crying after a game.

He asked, "Joe, do you think we'll ever win another game?"

At times, it seemed like a valid question.

Their average home attendance was 3,518 fans—lowest in the NBA.

In 1970–71, the average NBA crowd was 7,648. Fellow expansion teams Buffalo (4,977) and Portland (6,135) easily out-drew the Cavs.

The Cavs supposedly had 1,500 season tickets. Their lowest announced attendance was 1,737 vs. Portland.

But Tait and others are certain the Cavs inflated attendance figures to even reach the 3,518 level.

It was a scary time.

Most of the players were marginal talents hoping to find a way to stay in the NBA. Tait and others with the Cavs needed a job to support their families.

"Mileti told us he had no one," said Tait. "No one was showing up. Fitch kept hoping we'd get the first pick in the (1971) draft, and we did. No one was sure if we'd be back next season."

Fitch said he knew the team would return for another season. There was enough in the budget for that to happen.

"And I knew they'd never fire me," he said. "Who else would have wanted that job?"

The Cleveland Arena and the Early Years

It was either 1971 or '72. As a 10-year-old, I was at my first NBA game with my dad. It was the Cavs against the great Lakers team. After the game, we took the elevator down to the bottom floor, and at our first stop, the door opened and Wilt Chamberlain got on and stood next to me. I have never seen someone so big. He had his full uniform on and said he was going across the street to shower at the hotel.

—*Bob Rowland, Parma, Ohio*

During the initial losing streak, The Plain Dealer had a contest—predict the first-ever Cavs victory and win game tickets. And guess what? I won, and as a kid who did not have much, this was really fantastic. The tickets were for the game that ended up being the Cavs' first-ever home win. They gave every attendee free tickets to another game!

My brother and I were able to go down to the floor and snag a couple of autographs before a game. One time, we caught Larry Mikan on the way out after a game. He was very nice and polite, but couldn't understand why we would want his autograph. He was very accommodating as long as we would carry his bag out for him.

—*Greg Van Valkenburgh, North Royalton, Ohio*

The only game I ever went to at the Arena was a Cavaliers-Atlanta Hawks game Feb. 11, 1973. A couple high school teachers took me and a friend. The teachers knew some people with the Cavs, so we got a tour of some of the hockey locker rooms. The place was old but you could feel the history. The Cavs lost 115-107, and both Lou Hudson and Pete Maravich had big games. The most memorable part? It was the night of the famous Bill Fitch chair-throwing incident involving referee Bob Rakel.

—*Tim Lones, Massillon, Ohio*

The first season, a friend and I would go down to the Arena and get front row seats behind the Cavs bench for $6. We went to maybe 20 games, all really great seats.

—*Paul Korcuska, Parma Heights, Ohio*

Being born in February ruled out any possibility of my dad taking me to an Indians game on my birthday. But then the Cavs came along. For my 14th birthday, he treated me to a Cavs-Suns game. (Truth be told, I was more of a fan of Connie Hawkins than anyone on the Cavs' roster.) There was a noticeable ring of cigarette smoke whenever the lights went down in the Arena before the opening tip of a game. Also, there was a topless bar next door on Euclid Avenue. No, we never ventured inside!

—*Ken Hornack, Ormond Beach, Florida*

When Nick Mileti was awarded the NBA franchise, they offered stock to the public at $5 a share through a brokerage firm. I was a poor college student then and excited at the opportunity of owning a piece of a sports franchise. I only purchased 20 shares. I held them until the Gunds purchased the Cavs and all of the outstanding stock. I made a copy of the stock certificate as a souvenir. I remember we had the choice on the payout and I took four tickets offered in the lower bowl of the Coliseum.

I attended the first regular season home game, against the San Diego Rockets. Attendance that night was just over 6,000. I still have the program. They gave everyone in attendance drinking glasses that had the Cavalier on it with the motto, "Never Surrender No Matter What The Odds." I still have that.

—*Len Gold, Aurora, Ohio*

I drove three of my Lakewood High buddies down for a Cavs' rookies exhibition game versus Philadelphia in 1971. Austin Carr was the big attraction. This was his first public appearance in a Cavs uniform, I think, and he did not disappoint. His scoring was so easy and so smooth that I hardly even noticed that he was piling up the points. I think he finished with about 30 (editor's note: press reports said Carr had 32 points), but it was the most unpretentious 30 ever.

I got a flat tire on Baltic Avenue on the way home, and when I discovered the Ford Falcon's spare was also flat I had to sheepishly call my father to come rescue us. But it was another great memory of that old dump, the Cleveland Arena.

—*Mark Latvala, Emsworth, Pennsylvania*

When I was in high school in the 1960s, my father would take my friend and me to watch the Cincinnati Royals play some of their home games at the Arena. We always had great seats, and saw all the greats— Russell, Chamberlain, West and Baylor, Thurmond, etc. The teams stayed across the street at a hotel and walked over before game time in their uniforms and trench coats. We used to stand out front and watch them.

—*David Barnes, Wooster, Ohio*

I remember going to a Harlem Globetrotters game at the Cleveland Arena. The biggest takeaway was the smell of leather coats.

—*Allen Moebius, Spokane, Washington*

In high school, one of my basketball teammates' dads took our whole team from Erie, Pa., to watch the Cavs. I was 15. I remember looking around the old Arena, sitting in the upper deck and thinking the colleges in Erie had a better place to play than the Cavs did.

—*Tom Yochim, Erie, Pennsylvania*

CHAPTER 9

He Could Have Been a Hall of Famer

I remember watching Austin Carr on television a few times when he was with Notre Dame. He was the best college basketball player I'd ever seen, with Pete Maravich being a close second.

Of course, I'm thinking back to 1970. I was 15 years old. I had not watched a lot of college basketball. Nor was there a lot of college basketball on national television to be watched.

Now, Austin Carr is on television at least 100 times a year. He's an analyst for all 82 Cavs games. He also appears on pre- and-postgame shows. He is a regular guest on various radio and television sports talk shows.

We hear a lot from Austin Carr.

That amuses Joe Tait, who recalled interviewing Carr during the 1971–72 season. Carr was a rookie, and seemed in awe of Joe Tait.

"You could see that Bill Fitch and the players respected him," said Carr. "I made friends in Cleveland and they loved him as a broadcaster. In my mind, he was a big deal, even back then."

Tait was only in his second season broadcasting the Cavs games on radio, but Carr was a shy rookie who was drilled with this mindset: "Rookies are to be seen and not heard."

That could help a younger player blend in with veterans on the roster, but it was painful for Tait.

"He gave one word answers," said Tait. "I used to tape a 7-minute

Bill Fitch had his eye on Austin Carr in the college draft.
"I knew he was a player who could change our franchise.
He also was a great kid." *The Cleveland Press Collection, Michael
Schwartz Library, Cleveland State University*

interview for halftime. I ended up talking for about 6 minutes and
30 seconds. Austin couldn't even fill 30 seconds."

Tait laughed.

"The next year I interviewed him, I couldn't shut him up," Tait
said. "And he's been talking ever since."

* * *

One advantage to the Cavs' dismal 15-67 first-year record was
that they ended up with the No. 1 pick in the 1971 NBA draft.

"You know how I found out I was drafted by the Cavs?" asked
Carr.

OK, how?

"I was in history class at Notre Dame," said Carr. "My professor told me what happened. Cleveland had picked me. Later, my agent called. I don't even remember hearing from the Cavaliers that day."

Now, not only is the NBA draft televised, but there is a separate ESPN show featuring the ping-pong ball lottery system to determine the draft order.

But in 1971 few NBA games were even on national TV. The draft was followed by only the hardest of hardcore fans. The top college players such as Carr knew it was coming, but it was not viewed as a life-changing event.

Consider that after Carr was told he was picked by the Cavs, he went to his next class.

This was the same Austin Carr who averaged 38.1 points a game as a junior for Notre Dame. He came back as a senior and averaged 37.9 points per game.

"That was before the 3-point shot," said Carr. "I'd have averaged over 40 points easy with the 3-point line."

Carr smiled as he said it.

Not bragging, just mentioning it in passing.

Carr said older Cavs fans remember him as a player, a key part of the 1975–76 Miracle of Richfield team.

"But most people now know me from doing the games (Cavs TV broadcasts). They see me and say, 'GET THAT WEAK STUFF OUTTA HERE!'" Carr said, quoting one of his signature lines.

He has been doing the games on TV since 1999. He has been a part of the Cavaliers organization for 35 years.

His broadcasting partner, Fred McLeod (who died in 2019), called Carr "Mr. Cavalier."

He is all that—and more.

*   *   *

As the 1971 draft approached, Wayne Embry was in his first year as general manager of the Milwaukee Bucks. Coached by Larry Costello, the Bucks were the defending NBA champions. They had the No. 17 pick in the draft.

"Do I need to look at film of Carr?" asked Costello.

"No," said Embry.

"Why not?" asked the coach.

"Because we'll never get a shot at him," said Embry. "And if we do, you don't need to see film. We're taking him."

"He's that good?" asked Costello.

"No," said Embry. "He's great."

Embry recently recalled that conversation from 1971.

"If Austin Carr had stayed healthy, I have no doubt that he would have been a Hall of Famer," said Embry.

I recalled watching Carr score 46 points as Notre Dame upset UCLA in a nationally televised game. It was Jan. 23, 1971. It was the only game the Bruins would lose that season. This was during the days of black and white, three-channel television. It was when few games were broadcast. It was when most information on college players came from the newspapers, Sports Illustrated or Street & Smith's magazine.

It also was the most points ever scored by a player against a John Wooden-coached UCLA team. While it is a game that lives in Notre Dame history because UCLA was such a power, Carr had so many games like that.

"I saw him score 61 points against Ohio U.," recalled Tait, and that remains an NCAA tournament record.

But in his next NCAA game, Carr scored 52 against Adolph Rupp's powerhouse Kentucky team.

"Carr conducts a clinic on the court. He is the most outstanding player in the country this year," Rupp told reporters after Carr shredded his team's defense. "We put five different players on him and he still scored 50."

Carr scored 43 points in an 84-83 overtime regular season loss to South Carolina. He played all 45 minutes. He shot 19-of-24 from the field, 5-of-5 at the foul line and didn't commit a turnover.

"We tried every defense imaginable on Carr," said South Carolina coach Frank McGuire. "Nothing could stop him. Not man-to-man. Not zone. Not double-teaming. I've seen a lot of great ones and he is as good as any player I've ever seen."

Carr averaged 41.3 points in seven NCAA tournament games. He shot 51 percent from the field. He averaged 8.8 rebounds. The No. 2 all-time leading NCAA tournament career scorer is Bill Bradley, who averaged 33.7 points for Princeton. It's doubtful anyone will break Carr's NCAA tournament scoring average record.

"Someone once said no wonder I scored 61 (against Ohio)," said Carr. "After all, I took 44 shots. I did. But I made 25 of them."

The late 1960s and 1970s was an exciting time in college basketball, at least for young fans who loved stars scoring huge numbers.

From 1967–70, LSU's Pete Maravich averaged 44.2 points. He also unofficially led the nation in behind-the-back-passes, behind-the-back-dribbles and other plays that are common in the NBA now but seemed straight out of the Harlem Globetrotters during that era.

In the 1969–70 college season, Maravich averaged 44.5 points, followed by Carr (38.1) and Purdue's Rick Mount (35.4). A small college player—a 5-foot-9 guard from Kenyon College named John Rinka—averaged 41 points.

This was all before the 3-point shot.

In 1970–71, Carr averaged 38 points. But that wasn't enough to lead the nation. That honor belonged to a Mississippi player named Johnny Neumann, who averaged 40.1 points. He had an undistinguished career in the ABA.

Perhaps the most impressive part of Carr's game was his career shooting percentage—53 percent. It's not like he fired up an array of wild shots just to pad his scoring average. He played smart and in control. Sometimes he had to be told to shoot even more by Irish coach Johnny Dee.

Notre Dame had nice players such as Collis Jones and Sid Catlett, but Carr was the sun, moon and stars in the South Bend basketball galaxy. The team finished with a 20-9 record.

* * *

Fitch not only was the coach of the NBA expansion Cavaliers in 1971, he also was their general manager. He picked the players,

Austin Carr was a 6-foot-4 guard who could drive to the rim or stop 10-to-15 feet from the basket, then swish a jumper off the dribble. *The Cleveland Press Collection, Michael Schwartz Library, Cleveland State University*

coached the players and even negotiated the contracts for the players.

"I didn't need to talk to Austin before the draft," recalled Fitch. "I knew he was a player who could change our franchise. He also was a great kid."

Boston Celtics coach and GM Red Auerbach once told Milt Richman of UPI: "There are guards, then there's Austin Carr."

The top-rated players after Carr in the 1971 draft were UCLA's Sidney Wicks, Kentucky State's Elmore Smith and Ken Durrett, a forward from LaSalle.

Besides Carr, the only other player Fitch considered at No. 1 was Wicks, a 6-foot-8 forward for national champion UCLA.

"We're happy with Carr and we feel he suits our needs better than Wicks," Fitch told UPI's Milt Richman. "We were weakest at guard . . . Nobody has to throw the ball to Carr. He'll bring it down to the basket himself. Every time he does that, it's 20 points coming down the floor."

Fitch also praised Carr's character. He graduated with a degree in economics.

"We couldn't possibly ask for a better performer or more of an all-around high type individual than Austin Carr," said Fitch.

On the day of the draft, Fitch predicted Carr "would be a superstar."

Carr was a 6-foot-4 guard who could create his own shot by driving to the rim.

Or by stopping between 10-to-15 feet from the basket, then swishing a jumper off the dribble. Modern NBA analytics would hate his shot selection, but he was the master of the mid-range jumper.

He also could make shots from what is now 3-point range. He could score near the rim with either hand. He rarely took a bad shot. He was a respectable passer.

He is the greatest college player who seems to be lost in the pages of basketball history.

While writing this, I wondered what kind of pro career Wicks had. I knew he played for a long time.

Wicks was the No. 2 pick in the draft behind Carr. He played his first five seasons with Portland, averaging 22.3 points and 10.3 rebounds. His NBA career lasted 10 seasons, with a 16.8 scoring average and 8.7 rebounds. He made four All-Star teams.

*   *   *

Carr signed a five-year, $1.5 million contact with the Cavaliers—about $300,000 annually.

"I got a $7,500 signing bonus," he said. "I bought a purple Oldsmobile Toronado. That was when they put four lights in the back. I loved that car, but my mother hated it."

Why?

"I drove the car to her house and parked in the driveway," he said. "She asked where was my new car. I said it was in the driveway. It was purple with a white top and white tires."

Carr's mother stared at it, shook her head and said: "Son, I did not raise a pimp. You get rid of that car tomorrow!"

The next day, Carr arranged for the dealership to come and tow away the car.

"I bought a classy Mercedes," he said.

His mother's reaction?

"Now you're talking," she said.

Carr came from a strict family. His parents were Catholic. That is why he went to Notre Dame. They demanded he stay in school for his senior year and graduate with a real degree—in economics.

"My father (Austin Carr Sr.) worked for the Navy Department near Washington (D.C)," said Carr. "He was in the supply department. He believed he could have been the head of the department, but it required a college degree. He didn't have one. He made sure his son got one. My mother (Lula Mae Carr) was a nurse. We were a middle class family and we watched how we spent our money—very tight."

Carr said the Notre Dame coaches promised his parents, "We will keep your son in line."

That was exactly what they wanted to hear.

*　　*　　*

In 2019, I called Fitch and asked him about Carr.

"If only he hadn't gotten hurt," he said.

After he signed with the Cavaliers, Carr played in two rookie league games.

"Austin hit for 51 points in 51 minutes," reported the Cavs 1971 media guide. "Then he suffered a broken bone in his right foot at the end of June."

Carr tried to come back too soon during training camp in the fall. He broke it again during the first week.

"I was cutting to the basket, just changing directions," he said. "It was during practice. No one touched me. It just broke. I guess it was wear-and-tear from playing on all those concrete playgrounds growing up."

Carr missed the first 39 games of his rookie season, but still averaged 21.2 points, shooting 43 percent from the field. When that year was over, he had bone graft surgery on that same foot.

"Typical Cavalier luck," said Tait, recounting what Fitch told him after Carr's rookie year injuries.

*   *   *

I know I've spent a lot of time discussing Carr's college career. That's because it's lost in history. We never saw that Austin Carr with the Cavaliers.

This is not to say Carr could have been another LeBron James. He didn't have the same 6-foot-8 size, incredible strength and athleticism as the Cavs' all-time great.

But could Carr have been another Jerry West? I don't think that's a huge stretch,

Carr averaged 21 points over his first three Cavs seasons. He made the 1974 All-Star team. He was a good player, but lacked the explosive first step and athleticism he'd displayed in college.

His first foot surgery was a "fusion . . . they took a bone from my hip and put it into my foot."

The foot never had the same mobility as before the injury.

By his third season, Carr was having knee problems. He had knee surgery in his fourth year.

"It was the same right leg as the foot injuries," said Carr. "I ended up having four knee surgeries before I retired. I had to learn how to play with pain. I had no real cartilage in the knee in my last five years. There were days when it felt like my knee had rocks in it. One day, I jumped, came down and my knee cap was pointing to the right."

Carr said he had to alter his jump shot so he would not land hard on his right knee.

"After I retired, I had my knee replaced," he said. "The doctor said, 'I don't know how you played on this.' I told him that I didn't know, either."

Carr said he took about 30 pounds of weights on the road.

"When I got to my hotel room, I did leg lifts with them to keep them strong," he said. "This was before teams had weight rooms and conditioning coaches. My teammates would go out to dinner, I did leg exercises. The same thing at home, leg lifts in front of the TV—so I could watch and work out at the same time."

Carr doesn't like to talk about the injuries or the frustration he felt. He played 11 years and averaged 15.4 points. He made one All-Star team.

"When I think about it, I've been blessed," he said. "The Cavs and the fans have been super to me."

His No. 34 is retired and hangs in the rafters at Rocket Mortgage FieldHouse, formerly Quicken Loans Arena, in downtown Cleveland.

He doesn't look back often at his career.

"A lot of younger fans don't even know I played," he said. "They know me from watching the games. I really don't have regrets."

But he did when Fitch was elected to the Hall of Fame in 2019.

Carr sent him a note of congratulations, and added, "I just wish I could have been the player for you that you drafted."

CHAPTER 10

A Miracle? Yes, It Was!

If you grew up during the LeBron James Era of Cavalier basketball, the Miracle of Richfield means nothing to you.

Even if someone who was there tried to explain what it was like in 1976 . . .

Someone who remembers their head *splitting*, their ears *ringing* and the chants of "LET'S GO CAVS . . . LET'S GO CAVS!"

Someone who will never forget how the fans *roared* for a half-hour before a game when the team took the court for pregame layups . . .

Someone who was in the Cavaliers locker room during a pregame talk and remembers the blackboard *shaking* when coach Bill Fitch was drawing up plays as the team was preparing to take the court for the second half . . .

Someone who listened to games on the radio and remembers Joe Tait *screaming* in the final moments of big games . . .

"It was deafening," said Rick Hofacker. "That was my first year with the Cavaliers, and I've been with the team ever since. I never heard anything that loud."

Hofacker was a 16-year-old Cavaliers ball boy during the 1975–76 season.

A miracle?

Yes, it was . . . in its own way.

Time for a little history lesson.

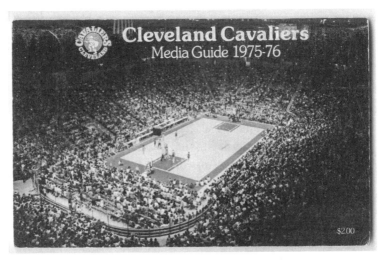

The Cavaliers media guide for the Miracle year shows a crowded Coliseum. That season, the crowds would get bigger—and louder. "It was deafening," recalls former ball boy Rick Hofacker. *Author's collection*

The season before the miracle (1974–75) saw the Cavaliers miss the playoffs by a game. They had a 40-42 record.

The Cavs' final game of the season was against the Kansas City-Omaha Kings. Let's stop right there. The franchise really was based in Kansas City, Missouri, AND Omaha, Nebraska. That's right, they split games in two different cities . . . in two different states.

This franchise was the old Cincinnati Royals, the same Cincinnati Royals who played some games in Cleveland in the late 1960s. They moved to Kansas City-Omaha in 1972. The franchise later moved to Sacramento.

That history lesson shows the precarious nature of pro basketball in the 1960s, 1970s and early 1980s. The Cavs weren't the only franchise losing money.

The date was April 6, 1975. The place was Omaha. The Cavs were trailing 95-94 in the final seconds of the game. The Cavs had the ball. If the Cavs won, they made the playoffs.

"Fitch drew up a play for almost anyone on the court to shoot except Freddie Foster," said Tait. "So you know what happened. The ball ended up in the hands of Foster."

Foster averaged 6.9 points that season.

Here is how Tait described the final play on the radio: "This has been a season of struggle . . . a season of injuries . . . a season of comebacks . . . three seconds left. Who will take the last shot? (Jim) Cleamons throws it to Foster at the foul line. He shoots. Blocked. And the Cavs season ends in Omaha, Nebraska."

This was year five in the history of the franchise:

Year	Record	Average Home Attendance
1970–71	15-67	3,518
1971–72	23-59	5,222
1972–73	32-50	4,548
1973–74	29-53	4,013
1974–75*	40-42	8,161

First season at Richfield Coliseum

"Making it worse, Buffalo made the playoffs," said Tait. "They came into the NBA with us as an expansion team."

*   *   *

Fitch was still serving as general manager/coach as the 1975-76 season opened. Owner Nick Mileti was not interested in firing (and paying off) Fitch. Mileti had been very busy raising the cash to build the Richfield Coliseum.

Mileti had little encouragement from the city of Cleveland to build a new downtown arena. The city was on its way to a financial crisis. In 1978, Cleveland defaulted on $15.5 million in debts.

Meanwhile, Mileti continually found ways to entice new investors and loans.

By the summer of 1975, he had done the following:

1968: Bought the old Cleveland Arena and the minor league Cleveland Barons hockey team for $1.8 million.

1970: Bought the Cavaliers for $3.7 million.

1972: Bought the Cleveland Indians for $10 million.

1972: Bought the Cleveland Crusaders hockey team for $120,000.

1972: Bought radio stations WWWE (now WTAM) and WWWM for $3.5 million.

1975: Built the Richfield Coliseum for $36 million.

Always remember Mileti operated with Other People's Money. He had investors, including 54 different ones at one point in his ownership of the Tribe. He had loans. He never owned more than 10% of the Cavaliers or Indians, according to a Sports Illustrated story by Jerry Kirshenbaum.

In a July 3, 1973, Plain Dealer story, Hal Lebovitz wrote:

> The gangsters who occupy the bar stools at some of our town's better taverns have come up with a Mileti Cocktail. It works this way: The gent who orders one throws down a quarter for the ginger ale, and everyone else is supposed to buy a whiskey for him . . . The Mileti Cocktail gag is an outgrowth of his own actions. Nick provides the token two bits and somehow cons everybody else into putting up the rest while he savors the drink. That's the way it seems to the public, and that's not far from the truth.

But the fact is Mileti somehow found a way to own all those teams . . . and the old arena . . . and the radio stations . . . and build a new arena.

He got things done at a time when Northeast Ohio was bleeding jobs and residents. It was an era when the city and county governments seemed paralyzed.

Mileti found a way to privately build the Coliseum in Richfield. He had this vision of Cleveland and Akron becoming one metropolis. His research revealed 4.7 million people lived within an hour drive of Richfield, 2.8 million within a half-hour. And the Coliseum was right off Interstate 271, not far from Interstates 77 and 71. He believed hotels and shopping malls would soon grow up around the Coliseum.

According to a Plain Dealer story by Amos Kermisch, Mileti took out loans from Chase Manhattan and Mellon banks for almost all of the $32 million purchase price. The Plain Dealer reported the loan was "at least 4 percent over prime," meaning an interest rate of about 14% in the middle 1970s. That came to about $3.7 million in annual payments to handle the interest.

But somehow, the Coliseum arose from what was once farm land. It was a spectacular facility for its time, even if many fans considered it in the middle of nowhere. The new building had about 20,000 seats for basketball. There were about 300 events—concerts, hockey and basketball games, the circus and ice shows—held most years.

That itself seemed almost a miracle—how did he ever get the thing built with so little cash? Well, he made it work.

Mileti also helped Tait become a local media star. Remember, he owned the radio flagship station (WWWE) for the Indians and Cavaliers, and Tait did play-by-play for both franchises. Tait was a small-town radio guy in 1970 when hired to do the Cavs games. He wondered if he'd ever achieve his dream of calling big league sports.

And he did—for two teams.

Another miracle.

In February 1974, Mileti secured another $2 million loan to make payroll and keep the Cavaliers operating. That was on top of the $32 million for the new Coliseum.

According to a May 25, 1975, Plain Dealer story by Amos Kermisch, the Indians lost $2.8 million in the first three years of Mileti's ownership. The hockey Crusaders lost $1.2 million in their first season. The Cavs lost $779,000 in their first four years at the old Cleveland Arena.

Why detail all of Mileti's financial dealings?

Because it's part of the miracle story.

How did he ever buy all these teams? How did he keep them in business? How did he ever get the Richfield Coliseum built?

*   *   *

Clockwise from top left: Nate Thurmond (defending Kareem Abdul-Jabbar); Jim Cleamons (driving past Bill Walton); Campy Russell; Jim Chones. "They played beautiful team basketball," recalled Joe Tait. *The Cleveland Press Collection, Michael Schwartz Library, Cleveland State University*

That was the sports landscape as the Cavs opened the 1975–76 season. The team had the legitimate expectation of making the playoffs. The losing had allowed them to pick high in the draft. Their choices were:

1970: John Johnson, No. 7 overall.

1971: Austin Carr, No. 1 overall.

1972: Dwight Davis, No. 3 overall.

1973: Jim Brewer, No. 2 overall.

1974: Campy Russell, No. 8 overall.

1975: John Lambert, No. 15 overall.

So the Cavs had three picks in the top three from 1971 to 1973. They also acquired 6-foot-10 Jim Chones, a 24-year-old promising big man from the old American Basketball Association.

But the Cavs opened the 1975–76 season with a 6-11 record.

"Guys were mad at Fitch," recalled Chones. "They thought they weren't getting enough shots and playing time."

Some players believed the offense was too structured. Other had simply grown weary of Fitch's "Marine-like" coaching style. Several people around the team characterized Fitch's personality that way—at least during his early years.

That's when Fitch made a deal that changed the season, on Nov. 27, 1975.

The Chicago Bulls thought the 34-year-old Nate Thurmond was nearing the end of his career. He had cranky knees. He had a painful hammer toe. The Bulls felt he was too expensive and just wanted to dump him. Fitch sent backups Steve Patterson and Eric Fernsten to Chicago for backup forward Rowland Garrett and Thurmond.

Thurmond was raised in Akron and played for Central High and later Bowling Green. He also was a seven-time All-Star by the time he was dealt to the Cavs.

"The trade changed everything," said Tait. "We'd never had a player like him before."

Ball boy Hofacker was in the locker room when Thurmond arrived. He said many of the players sort of stared at the 6-foot-11 center.

"They knew a Hall of Famer had just walked through the door," said Hofacker. "It was like they were a little in awe of him."

Hofacker heard one of the first team meetings involving Thurmond.

Fitch had given the usual post-game talk after a loss.

As Hofacker recalled, Thurmond stood up and said, "Coach, can I say something?"

Fitch agreed.

"Nate looked at Chones and said he didn't come to take away his starting (center) job," said Hofacker.

Chones was worried about that.

Then Thurmond talked about the need for team unity. Guys had to stop worrying about starting. They needed to cheer for each other when they came out of the game.

"This should be a very good team," Thurmond said. "The talent is here. We just need to play together."

No doubt, Fitch had emphasized many of the same themes when talking to the team.

"But coming from Nate, it was different," said Tait. "Because of Nate's stature as a player, it had more power."

Tait admitted he didn't know if Thurmond could be a factor. Word in the NBA was Thurmond's knees were like broken glass inside. He was averaging only 3.7 points and 5.5 rebounds in 20 minutes per game for the Bulls at the time of the deal.

But the trade to Cleveland seemed to not only energize the Cavs, but also Thurmond. The Akron native appreciated a chance to play near his hometown, even though he had moved to San Francisco.

Thurmond also knew with his fragile knees, his NBA time was short. He had to cherish every moment of what remained of his career.

*   *   *

With the great Nate Thurmond willing to come off the bench, how could Campy Russell complain about not starting?

Or Austin Carr?

Or anyone else in Cavalier wine and gold?

"The fans immediately embraced Nate," recalled Tait. "When he'd come off the bench, they'd roar as he went to the scorer's table—waiting to get into the game."

Carr was coming off one of his knee surgeries. He wanted to start. When healthy, Carr was a superior player to veteran shooting guard Dick Snyder. But Carr wasn't healthy.

Besides, the Cavs second unit became a force. Thurmond was the engine. He blocked shots. He battled opposing centers. He came onto the court, his shoulder slightly slumped. He wore huge knee pads. You knew the man ached when he moved after 13 years and more than 36,000 minutes on the court.

"We became a well-oiled machine after the trade," said Carr. "Everybody knew exactly what they were supposed to do at both ends of the court."

Chones and Russell talked about the team becoming "unselfish." With Thurmond setting a physical example of how to defend opposing centers, starter Chones committed himself to doing the same.

That team with its 6-11 record went 43-22 after Thurmond arrived. No matter how cranky his knees were or how much his back ached, Thurmond played every single game for the Cavs after the deal.

The Cavs leading scorer was Chones (15.8 points), the starting center. The second-leading scorer was Russell (15.0 points), a second-year pro who was a physically gifted 6-foot-8 small forward.

The Cavs had seven different players averaging between 10 and 15.8 points. It was a balanced scoring team, a true team.

*   *   *

It's doubtful a player the caliber of Russell would be willing to come off the bench now. He was among the nation's top five high school players and the Michigan High School Player of the Year in 1970 at Pontiac Central High. He averaged 30.2 points and 12.6 rebounds.

Russell attended the University of Michigan, where he played on the freshman team in his first season. This was when freshmen didn't play varsity because of NCAA rules.

He then spent two years on the varsity. In his second varsity season, he averaged 23.7 points and 11.1 rebounds. The Cavs were overjoyed when he dropped to them at No. 8 in the draft.

The Cavs actually had the No. 3 pick in the 1974 draft. They knew Seattle liked 7-foot-3 Tom Burleson. This was when big men were valued—the bigger, the better. Fitch believed he had his center in Chones. So he sent the No. 3 pick to Seattle and received the No. 8 pick, veteran guard Dick Snyder and $250,000.

Given the mediocre career of Burleson, the deal became a steal for the Cavaliers.

"No one from Cleveland talked to me before the draft," said Russell. "When I was drafted, the Cavs, they talked to my agent. They never talked to me."

This was long before the NBA draft was televised with the top college players present in New York, waiting for their names to be called. It was before each team brought its top recently drafted players to town for press conferences.

"I never met Bill Fitch until training camp opened," said Russell.

That was in the fall of 1974. He was going to a team that had a 29-53 record.

Russell thought there would be plenty of playing time available. He was a college star, an elite scorer. The Cavs were a losing team.

"About two weeks into camp, Fitch said he didn't plan to play me much," said Russell.

Fitch explained he already had four forwards for two spots: Jim Brewer, Bingo Smith, Dwight Davis and Freddie Foster.

"But Coach, you haven't really seen me play," Russell told Fitch. "The veterans haven't even come in yet. You haven't seen me play against them. You don't know what I can do."

Fitch had little interest in Russell's opinion.

"That's my plan," the coach said. "I'm going to bring you along slow."

As a rookie, Russell played in only 68 of 82 games. He averaged 11.1 minutes and 6.2 points.

"I was watching all these guys drafted before and after me playing a lot more than me," he said. "It was frustrating. I was like WOW . . . I know I'm better than some of those guys."

After the 1974–75 season, Fitch traded Foster and Davis to create room for Russell to receive regular duty coming off the bench.

In the Miracle season, he averaged 15 points, 4.2 rebounds and shot .482 from the field. He scored those 15 points in 24 minutes a game.

He was the most naturally gifted scorer on the team.

The Cavs' first four players off the bench were point guard Foots Walker, Russell (forward), Carr (shooting guard) and Thurmond (center).

Most teams are happy if they don't lose ground on the scoreboard when they bring in their reserves. The Cavs often went into a higher gear. Carr and Russell supplied the scoring. Walker set up the offense and was a pesky defender against opposing point guards.

Thurmond rebounded, defended and inspired.

Fitch often kept one of his starters on the court with that group.

The 1975–76 Cavs committed the fewest turnovers in the NBA. They ranked No. 2 in fewest points allowed, the defense holding the opposition to 99 per game.

"They played beautiful team basketball," recalled Tait. "Nate would play the last 8-10 minutes of each half, when it meant the most. He was the heart and soul of the team."

In the final two months of the regular season, the Cavs became a hot ticket. The Coliseum parking lot was jammed. After games, fans sat in their cars, stuck in the parking lot, listening to Pete Franklin's post-game show from a glass-enclosed booth in the Coliseum.

"The players listened, too," said Chones. "Sometimes, I stuck around after the game and talked to Joe and Pete on the air."

If Nate Thurmond was the heartbeat, Tait and Franklin were the soundtrack of that remarkable season.

A winning team generated attention. Billboards and a theme song helped, too. Plus, the Cavs had affordable tickets and a roster of likable players. "Fans felt like they knew us," Campy Russell said. *The Cleveland Press Collection, Michael Schwartz Library, Cleveland State University*

Disc jockey Larry Morrow supplied a theme song: "Come on Cavs, Gotta Make it Happen!" It had a Motown beat.

The dungeon of the old Arena and the embarrassment of being one of the NBA's worst franchises was gone. Up rose this stunning basketball palace in Northeast Ohio farmland. It had a team that was so good, yet didn't have a single player make the All-Star Game. That's because they were a team, not a star-driven basketball stage show.

Yes, a miracle.

*   *   *

For the 1976 playoffs, $12.50 was the price for a floor seat. For $7.50 or $6, you could sit in the lower bowl. There were $5 tickets for general admission in the upper bowl.

"The average fan could not only afford to come to the game, he could sit near the court," said Hofacker.

They often were as excited and wide-eyed as the rookie ball boy for 1975–76.

I'm quoting Hofacker because the Akron St. Vincent-St. Mary High junior had his own miracle story.

The Akron Beacon Journal ran a contest to pick ball boys. Hofacker entered hoping to snare some of the free tickets they also were giving away.

He had just been cut from his high school basketball team "for the third time in three years," recalled Hofacker. He came home and his mother told him that he'd won the ball boy contest.

He showed up and they handed him a mop. He sat under the basket for the opener against Golden State. Whenever a player fell on the court or an official spotted water, he was brought on the court during a timeout to mop it up.

In the dressing room, he picked up "socks, jocks, uniforms and towels." He made sure Bingo Smith had his favorite socks, "ones with lots of elastic." After a while, he was moved to the bench. He handed towels and water to players.

"Chones never drank water during games," said Hofacker. "That was back when you weren't supposed to drink water when playing."

Hofacker winces as he thinks about how players shared towels.

"One guy would have the flu, another guy would grab his towel," he said. "Then that guy would get sick. Before you knew it, half the team had the flu."

Hofacker helped trainer Charlie Strasser. He remembered equipment manager Andy Bell taping the games with an old movie camera, then setting them up for the team to watch on a reel-to-reel projector.

"Jimmy Rodgers was the only assistant coach," said Hofacker. "He also was the chief scout. Sometimes, he was on the road and that meant Bill Fitch was the only coach on the bench."

One day, Fitch was ejected. The coach trudged to the locker room. A few minutes later, the trainer told Hofacker, "Go see Bill."

Hofacker found Fitch in the locker room. He handed the 16-year-old a piece of paper with a play drawn up, with these orders: "Take this to Bingo."

Hofacker returned to the bench. There was a timeout. He handed the play to Bingo Smith, who showed it to the players and said, "This is what we'll do."

Cavs ball boys present Austin Carr with a cake. Rick Hofacker (third from right) won a contest to become a ball boy—a job he held from 1975 to 1987, while attending college and podiatry school. After graduating, he became the team's podiatrist. *Courtesy of Rick Hofacker*

"Can you imagine anything like that happening now?" Hofacker asked.

In a word . . . No.

This was a different time, a different place and a different view of the world. Pro athletes were still a special class, but far more accessible.

"We connected with the fans," said Russell.

The players parked in the same lot as the fans and walked through the Coliseum concourse, then outside to their cars. They met fans. They shook hands. They signed autographs.

"We were approachable," said Russell. "Fans felt like they knew us, and we got to know a lot of them."

Tait and others talk about how the fans didn't need a scoreboard or cheerleaders to "GET LOUD" as you often hear now.

"It just happened," said Tait. "It was genuine. It was a dream season. Nate Thurmond came home to lead us out of the wilderness. Fans exploded every time he came off the bench. No marketing agency could create it because it was real."

*   *   *

The Cavs won the Central Division and made the playoffs for the first time in their history. Their 49-33 record was the second best in the Eastern Conference, behind Boston (54-28).

They faced Washington in a best-of-7 conference semifinal series.

This was a different era. Only five teams in each conference made the playoffs—a total of 10.

Not like now when 16 teams are in the postseason.

The Washington series was stunning because the games were so close, the crowds so huge, the sizzle so new for Cavs fans. This was the first playoff appearance in franchise history.

The Cavs won it in seven games.

Here were the final scores of their victories: 80-79, 88-76, 92-91 and 87-85.

Three of the four wins were by one or two points! Tait seemed to be screaming for two hours each night on the radio.

Here were the attendance figures for the four games at the Coliseum:

19,974

21,061

21,312

21,564.

It's still hard to imagine where they put more than 21,000 fans in a building with about 19,500 actual seats for basketball.

Hardcore Cavs fans then know what happened.

The Cavs were set to play Boston in the Eastern Conference Finals.

"I can still see it," said Fitch. "It was our last practice before the Boston series. Chones came down with a rebound . . . "

"I heard a snap," said Chones. "I thought I broke my foot."

It was a stress fracture.

Dick Snyder hits the game-winner against the Washington Bullets in Game 7 of the Miracle in Richfield on April 29, 1976, at the Coliseum. It was the franchise's first-ever playoff series win. *Paul Tepley, special to The Plain Dealer*

No Chones for the next round.

Thurmond took over at center and went from playing 17 minutes a game to 37 against the Celtics. He averaged 10.5 points and 10.7 rebounds. Boston needed six games to beat the Cavs, but the dreams of a title were fractured when Chones broke his foot.

"We would have won the title that year," said Tait. "No question in my mind."

Russell, Carr and Chones all said the same thing. Fitch remains convinced of it.

Even miracles often come with a time limit.

*   *   *

But the miracle lives on in Austin Carr, who serves as an analyst for the current Cavs games on TV.

It lives on in Jim Chones, who has the same type of job as Carr, on the Cavs radio broadcasts.

It lives on in Campy Russell, who works on the Cavs post-game TV shows.

It lives on in the memory of fans, who can still hear Tait's calls of those games.

"I've had some people say I made the miracle year," said Tait. "It made me."

It lives on in Hofacker, who was a ball boy from 1975 to 1987. He did it through college and podiatry school. He graduated on May 31, 1987. He then became the team's podiatrist, a job he still holds.

"I sometimes wonder what would have happened if I had not won that contest," said Hofacker. "It changed my life."

Miracles are made of stories like these. They seem to come out of nowhere. They bring incredible joy. When they are gone, you close your eyes and wonder, "How did that ever happen?"

And then, you smile and give thanks.

CHAPTER 11

Ted Stepien: It Wasn't Funny!

Now, some of the stories from the Ted Stepien Era are funny.

There was Ted Stepien dropping softballs from the top of the Terminal Tower in downtown Cleveland on June 24, 1980, hoping members of his professional softball team would catch them.

But one hit a woman, breaking her wrist. Another man was hit in the shoulder. Stepien plunked a car, denting the hood.

He had a polka for the team fight song, spending $5,000 to have it produced.

He created a semi-sleazy dance team called "The Teddi Bears." He hosted lingerie shows in a place called "The Competitors Club," a bar he owned in Cleveland. He helped pick the 33 "dancers."

"I may not be able to run a basketball team, but I can run a lingerie show," he told people attending one of his shows.

Stepien had a big guy named Don "Boot" Buttrey who was known as Fat Man Eating Beer Cans. He indeed bit into beer cans. He also ate raw eggs and stuffed donuts in his mouth.

Now that's entertainment.

I saw Buttrey's act at midcourt during a few games. People didn't know how to respond when he tore open a can with his teeth, holding a piece in each hand.

The fans just stared and seemed to be thinking, "Did that guy actually bite into a can? If so, why?"

I met Boot a few times. Nice guy.

But that wasn't true of Stepien, who spent $2.4 million to purchase controlling interest in the Cavs in 1980.

He told the media: "It's a fact having more white players would be beneficial from a marketing standpoint. But if we have 11 blacks and win a title, that's great."

Stepien hired Bill Musselman, perhaps the most reviled basketball coach in Northeast Ohio at the time. Musselman was coaching the University of Minnesota when several of his players attacked Ohio State center Luke Witte and other Buckeye players during a game. That was on Jan. 25, 1972. Eight years later, many fans in Northeast Ohio still remembered the ugly event.

When Musselman left Minnesota to coach in the American Basketball Association, the NCAA hit his college program with about 100 violations. You could not have picked a coach who would alienate more Cavs fans.

Musselman ended up with the Cavaliers because the coach convinced Billy Martin—the manager of the New York Yankees—to call Stepien and put in a good word for him. Musselman was coaching a minor league basketball team in Reno. He became friends with Martin, who liked to hit the casinos.

Stepien loved the fiery Billy Martin. He talked to Musselman, who had the ability to sell himself and explain and excuse his past indiscretions.

In his first Cavs preseason game, Musselman played veteran Randy Smith all 48 minutes. No one plays anyone—much less a veteran—all 48 minutes in the preseason. I saw another preseason game when he played Bill Laimbeer all 48 minutes.

NBA people and the players saw that and figured the coach had lost his basketball sanity. Musselman said he wanted to get his players into shape. Forty-eight minutes in the preseason was a great way to get his players hurt.

Under his watch, Musselman traded first-round picks from 1983 to 1986. He was trading away the team's ability to add talent for years in the future.

Expansion franchise Dallas ended up with Cavs first round

Cavs owner Ted Stepien, left, with coach Bill Musselman during the 1982 college draft. The two would trade away the Cavs' first-round picks from 1983 to 1986, ruining the franchise and leading to the NBA's "Stepien Rule".
Richard T. Conway / The Plain Dealer

picks from 1983 to 1986. The Cavs received the following in return: Jerome Whitehead, Geoff Huston, Richard Washington and Mike Bratz. All were marginal players.

By Nov. 28, 1980, the NBA stepped in and ruled it had to approve any trades made by the Cavs. The NBA believed the deals were ruining the franchise.

That later led to the "Stepien Rule," where the NBA decreed a team must have a first-round pick at least every other season.

Stepien and Musselman battled with the media. They alienated Joe Tait, the revered voice of the franchise. After one year, Tait left town for a job calling the New Jersey Nets games.

The local media promoted Tait's final home game of the 1980–81 season as a tribute to the broadcaster. The game on March 27, 1981 drew a season-high 20,175.

Much of the night, fans chanted, "WE WANT JOE, TED MUST GO!"

It was yet another deplorable episode, fans throwing food and screaming obscenities at Stepien, who was at the game.

The franchise was on financial life-support when Stepien purchased it. The NBA was having a hard time drawing fans. The national television networks had very little interest in the pro game. Some NBA Finals games in the late 1970s and early 1980s were shown on tape delay.

I become angry writing this because I was around for it. I was the baseball beat writer for The Plain Dealer, but I loved pro basketball. My wife and I would go to the games where there were sometimes no more than 1,000 fans in the 20,000-seat Coliseum. The franchise not only was a joke, it was a disaster.

You could not have designed a better game plan to have a franchise removed from a city than the one Stepien blundered into with his own insecurity and bullheadedness.

The great radio talk show host Pete Franklin used to call him "T.S., as in Too Stupid."

On Jan. 20, 1983, Stepien was on a radio station in Toronto, talking about moving the Cavs franchise to that city. Franklin found out about it, disguised his voice and called the station to talk to Stepien. He got through and berated Stepien on Canadian radio.

And it started with how he bought the franchise.

My father used to say, "How could you be that dumb?" when someone did something . . . well . . . really dumb.

During the Stepien Era, fans were saying something like that nearly every week.

*   *   *

On June 30, 1979, Sheldon Ocker of the Akron Beacon Journal reported the Cavs lost $720,103. They lost another $900,592 by the end of the 1979 calendar year.

Add it up, the losses were $1,620,695. Doesn't sound like much today.

But the Cavs were purchased for $3.7 million in 1970. In 1979, the Denver Nuggets were sold for about $2 million. The NBA was hurting in terms of attendance and image in the late 1970s. It was hard to find people willing to invest in some of the franchises.

Some strange business dealings ended with the dreaded Stepien owning the Cavaliers.

It began with some classic Nick Mileti business moves. As usual, they involved Other People's Money (OPM). When it comes to Mileti and business, OPM loomed over the situation—much like buzzards waiting for something bad to happen.

On Feb. 4, 1980, Mileti sold his 21% of the Cavaliers to Lou Mitchell.

Consider that after 10 years of "owning" the Cavs, Mileti's actual stake in the business was 21%. Mitchell had added shares from other part owners and became the Cavs' majority owner with 37%.

Mitchell didn't realize the dire financial situation of the franchise. A week after buying the controlling interest, he realized, "We couldn't meet the March payroll." He told the Beacon Journal he needed $200,000 in loans to cover expenses.

Thirty days after buying the team, Mitchell sold it to a man named Joe Zingale, who also was Mileti's cousin.

Mitchell estimated he lost about $1 million on the deal.

"I had to get out," he told the Beacon Journal.

Zingale reportedly paid $1.1 million for Mitchell's shares. Three weeks later, he sold them to Stepien for $2 million.

Mitchell never accused Zingale/Mileti of anything illegal.

How did Stepien become involved with the Tribe?

When Mileti owned the Indians, he had more than 40 minority partners. One of them was Stepien, who owned a highly successful company called Nationwide Advertising. It bought classified advertisements in newspapers across the country for companies looking for employees. So Mileti and Zingale knew Stepien had money. They also knew he was desperate to be a "player" in Cleveland pro sports. They reeled him in.

*   *   *

Writers Burt Graeff and Joe Menzer use about 15,000 words to cover the Stepien Era in detail in their excellent book, "Cavs From Fitch to Fratello." You can read many more deplorable Stepien and Musselman stories from those authors.

I'm not going to dwell on that dismal period.

But a couple of things are clear.

Stepien considered himself an outsider. He cherished his Polish heritage and he wanted to defy the "Dumb Pole" stereotype. He believed the Cleveland business and sports establishments didn't respect him.

It was easy for him to develop an affinity for Musselman, who also was disdained after all his problems at the University of Minnesota.

Now add in Don Delaney.

He was a friend of Stepien who also coached Stepien's pro softball team. To be fair to Delaney, he was a respected junior college basketball coach at Lakeland Community College, which is in suburban Cleveland. The Cavaliers sometimes spent part of their training camp at Lakeland, where Delaney got to know Cavs coach Bill Fitch and his staff.

But Delaney certainly was an NBA novice.

That didn't stop Stepien from making Delaney—get this—*general manager* of the NBA franchise.

Delaney's response was, "You want me to do what?"

"General manager," said Stepien.

It was too enticing for Delaney to turn down. He began coaching and teaching in high school. Then he was a small college coach. Now he could help Musselman assemble an NBA roster.

What started as a dream job became a nightmare for Delaney.

Of the three, Delaney was the best person and most mature. But all three—Stepien, Musselman and Delaney—had to feel like men sinking in a swamp dealing with NBA basketball.

I interviewed Musselman a few times over the years. Once when he was with the Cavaliers. The others were later when he was with the Minnesota Timberwolves and in the minor league Continental Basketball Association. Musselman could be charming and engaging when relaxed.

But this was a very insecure man. Then put him under the thumb of an insecure, impulsive owner with a mean streak. Add in Delaney, the general manager who knew he was not prepared for the job. Suddenly every day felt to Musselman like Game 7 of the NBA Finals. That led to all the panicked trading of draft picks to try to win right now.

Musselman coached parts of two seasons, where he had a 25-46 record in 1980–81 and then 2-21 in 1981–82. He would work in the front office with Stepien when not coaching during those seasons.

Delaney also took two turns at coaching: 3-8 in 1980–81 and 4-13 in 1981–82.

Stepien was going to show the NBA he could win with a disgraced coach (Musselman) and a junior college coach (Delaney) running the franchise.

In the middle of his second season, Stepien suddenly thought he needed someone else. He hired Chuck Daly, a veteran NBA assistant. Daly called the experience, "My 93 days at the Richfield Holiday Inn," where he lived in a hotel room.

Stepien/Musselman tested the strength of Daly's sanity. After a 9-32 record and 93 days, he was fired in the middle of the 1981–82 season. Musselman finished it out with that 2-21 record, including a 19-game losing streak.

Daly went on to become a Hall of Fame coach with Detroit, New Jersey and Orlando.

*   *   *

Before the 1982–83 season, Harry Weltman was hired as general manager. Weltman was the former general manager of the ABA's Spirits of St. Louis. He turned to Tom Nissalke as coach. That happened two weeks before the regular season.

Musselman's last draft was 1982. The Cavs took John Bagley in the first round and David Magley in the second round. Stepien was very amused by "Bagley & Magley" being the top two rookies whose names rhymed.

Bagley had a solid NBA career as a point guard. Magley played a grand total of 56 minutes with the Cavs.

Weltman fired Musselman after taking over the team in the middle of training camp. He also took over the drafting, although he kept the sincere and hard-working Delaney as part of the organization.

The NBA was pressuring Stepien to sell the team. He was on his way to losing about $20 million in his three years with the Cavs.

That sale eventually happened when Gordon Gund bought the Cavs in April 1983.

But after three years, Stepien left as a national basketball joke. The franchise was on the verge of moving to another city. It also was on the edge of a financial collapse. The fan base was sick of the team. The media was angry. Attacks on both sides (ownership and those covering the franchise) were personal and ugly.

Nothing funny about it, Cleveland pro basketball nearly died on Ted Stepien's watch.

CHAPTER 12

The Man Who Saved the Cavaliers

By the end of the Ted Stepien regime, the former Cavaliers owner was trying to move the franchise to Toronto . . . or somewhere.

This was 1983. The NBA was a distant third behind pro football and baseball in terms of fan interest. The league was still suffering poor television ratings. CBS cut the number of nationally televised regular-season games from 18 to four. ESPN was adding 40 games, but the cable network was still young.

The only good news for the NBA in the spring of 1983 was that CBS carried all the Finals games live, for the first time since 1978. The Philadelphia 76ers led by Julius Erving won the NBA title, and that sparked some interest.

In the 1982–83 season, the average NBA attendance was 10,220.

The Cavs' average announced attendance was 3,916, their lowest since the 1970–71 inaugural season (3,518). No one believed the 3,916 figure. It probably was closer to 2,000 per game.

"I know for a fact there were fewer than 1,000 people at several home games," said Gordon Gund.

How did he know that for a fact?

At that point, Gund owned the Coliseum. He bought it for a mere $300,000 in 1981. It had been built for $36 million seven years earlier. The building was a financial disaster and had reverted to mortgage holder Chase Bank in 1977. Early in his career, Gund had worked for "The Chase," as he called it, as an investment banker. "The Chase" was looking for someone to run the building.

I went to several games in that 1982–83 season. Free tickets were easy to find. Often, there were indeed fewer than 1,000 fans at the game. Many of them were there for free, just like my wife and me. The few people and businesses that had purchased tickets at the start of the season were dumping them.

It was almost an embarrassment to say you had bought a ticket to a Cavs game.

The NBA was begging Gund to take over the Cavaliers from Stepien. The league didn't want to lose the Cleveland market. For a long time, Gund insisted he wasn't interested.

But at one point, the league had a plan to combine the Cavaliers and the Indiana Pacers into one franchise headquartered in Indianapolis. The Pacers averaged only 4,814 fans in 1982–83. Maybe combining the two teams would upgrade the talent and create one respectable franchise. There was a legitimate fear the Stepien ownership had done so much damage in Cleveland the city could be ruined in terms of being a viable location for an NBA franchise.

The announced attendance for Cleveland's final four home games of the 1982–83 season:

2,441

2,039

1,952

2,495

The NBA knew the average attendance was closer to 2,000, not the announced 3,916. The NBA knew Stepien had lost about $20 million in his three seasons. The NBA knew it would require a massive influx of money and basketball brains to lead the franchise back to respectability.

"I can get the franchise for you cheap," NBA commissioner David Stern told Gund.

"Why would I want it?" Gund replied.

It was a good question.

When NBA commissioner David Stern told Gordon Gund he could get the Cavaliers franchise for cheap, Gund asked, "Why would I want it?" Fortunately for basketball fans in Northeast Ohio, Gund made a deal and kept the team in town. *Roadell Hickman / The Plain Dealer*

*   *   *

Gund was the most logical option for the NBA. Gund already owned the Richfield Coliseum. He needed basketball in his building, or at least that was what Stern believed.

But as Gund told me several years ago: "It would not have cost me that much to wrap up (close down) the building. I'd rather do that than buy something that was going to eat my lunch for years and years."

Gund's business career included looking for opportunities to buy "distressed properties," or companies in financial trouble. The goal is to nurture them back to financial health and perhaps sell them for a profit. Or keep them, if that seemed to be the wisest financial course.

But there also are times when it's better to "fold 'em," just shut down the business because the situation was financially terminal.

That was what Gund explained to Stern. Gund's point was the

franchise not only "was a mockery" in Cleveland, it had no chance to improve. The Stepien regime had traded all the first-round draft picks through the 1986 season. That meant for four years the NBA's worst franchise would have no first-round selections.

"Buying this right now is buying the right to lose money for a long time," Gund told Stern.

Stern realized Gund wasn't just talking tough to make a deal. The terms had to change or the Cavs could possibly fold.

Stern suggested the NBA might be willing to "sell" first-round picks to the Cavs in each of the next four years—1983–86. That was unprecedented. The league never wanted to reward teams for trading picks by allowing them to "buy" some more from the league. In certain circumstances, one team could trade and/or sell a draft pick to a different team.

Gund became interested, especially when he learned the NBA was ready to institute a salary cap in 1984. Finally, medium-sized markets such as the Cavaliers could have a better chance at keeping their own players headed to free agency. The first salary cap would limit payrolls to $3.6 million per team.

Stern said many of the other owners didn't like the idea of "giving" first-round picks to a franchise that had idiotically traded them all away. But Stern stressed doing so was good for the league, a league that absolutely had to get rid of Stepien.

In the end, Stern and Gund negotiated a deal whereby the Cavaliers could "buy" first-round picks in the next four years for a total of $1 million, or $250,000 each. It was a bargain.

But the sweetest deal for Gund came when he purchased the Cavs from Stepien.

Stepien was taking a financial bloodbath. Gund had an idea. He wanted more than the Cavaliers. He also wanted Stepien's Nationwide Advertising business. Now that enterprise was making money. Stepien wanted to keep Nationwide. But he also knew he couldn't financially survive another season owning the Cavaliers—even with Nationwide delivering profits.

Gund set up an offer where Stepien could "sell" the franchise for $20 million. That sounded very good.

But it also would include Nationwide Advertising. Nationwide had to be part of the deal, or no deal.

Stepien didn't like it. But what other option did he have?

Furthermore, Gund would pay $2.5 million up front. The next $17.5 million would be paid out over the next 10 years.

Gund's position was clear: If you don't like that offer, find a better one.

Stepien took it.

Over the next 10 years, much of the $17.5 million owed Stepien came from profits of Nationwide Advertising. Two years after Gund purchased the team, the Cavs made the 1985 playoffs.

Some fans can say Gund was purely a bottom-line guy who made several shrewd business investments with the Coliseum, the Cavaliers and Nationwide Advertising. There is no doubt these turned out to be very profitable for him.

What would have happened had Gund not bought the Cavaliers?

It's impossible to know, but probably they would not have remained in Cleveland. Stern would have either merged them with the Pacers, or found a buyer in another city willing to purchase the sad-sack franchise.

Suppose Gund had bought the Cavaliers without receiving the first-round picks?

Well, the 1983 purchased pick was Roy Hinson . . . who was later traded for the draft rights to Brad Daugherty.

In 1984, the pick was used as part of a deal for Mel Turpin. In 1985, the pick was part of a deal for Keith Lee.

In 1986, that pick became Ron Harper.

Not all the draft picks worked out, but Gund's maneuvering at least put the Cavaliers back in the game on draft day.

Most of all, Gund's deal revived the Cavaliers from near extinction to relevant and exciting within a few years.

CHAPTER 13

Why the Cavs Should Retire World B. Free's Number

Wayne Embry just didn't understand.

Or maybe, the former Cavs general manager didn't want to admit what World B. Free meant to the Cavaliers as they were coming out of the Ted Stepien Era.

Embry is an exceptional person. He was a good general manager for the Cavaliers and the Milwaukee Bucks. But when he came to the Cavaliers in the summer of 1986, one of his first big decisions was about re-signing Free.

Embry used to make fun of how the Cavaliers sent a helicopter to pick up Free at Burke Lakefront Airport on Sept. 30, 1983. Free was flown to the Richfield Coliseum, where a red carpet awaited him—leading the shooting guard to the door of the arena.

Why all the ceremony for player with a reputation for shooting too much, with the ball or his mouth?

The Cavaliers acquired Free from the Golden State Warriors on Dec. 15, 1982. They were the worst team in the NBA with a 3-19 record before he played his first game with his new team. Even worse, the Cavaliers were probably the most boring team to watch—dead last in the NBA in scoring. The few fans who did show up were there to scream that Stepien should sell the team.

Then came World B. Free.

"I remember when I got to the Cleveland airport right after the

The Cavs flew World B. Free from Burke Lakefront Airport to the Coliseum by helicopter and rolled out the red carpet—literally. He arrived in time for practice. *Plain Dealer staff*

trade," Free told me in 1986. "The people looked tired. I said I was going to pump some life into this place. 'What Cleveland needed was World B. shakin', bakin', stoppin' and poppin'. That's what I was thinking."

And there was more.

"When I got to the Coliseum, and wondered, where were all the people?" he said. "I remember there were games where the crowd was my girl and a couple of her friends. I'd try to give tickets away, and people would say, 'Hey, World, don't call me, I'll call you.' The team would walk through the airport and the baggage people would ignore us. It was sad."

Free changed some of that.

"I knew World's strengths and I knew his weaknesses," former Cavs general manager Harry Weltman told me years ago. "And I knew his strengths were what we needed. He could put the ball in the basket. He was exciting to watch. We desperately needed that."

Weltman didn't worry about Free forcing a few poor shots during a game. He inherited (from Bill Musselman) a roster full of guys who couldn't make wide open 15-footers . . . or guys who hated being in Cleveland.

Free was not a good defender, but he played hard. He signed autographs, posed for pictures, shook hands and made friends. Maybe he wasn't the brightest star in the NBA galaxy, but he was a ray of sunshine on the Cavaliers roster.

The Cavs finished the 1982–83 season with a 20-40 record after the Free trade. They were 3-19 before.

He averaged 24.2 points and shot .458 from the field. Free was a free agent in the summer of 1983. After Gordon Gund bought the team, he green-lighted a multi-year deal for Free. Weltman signed him with the help of team attorney and salary cap expert Richard Watson.

Weltman and Watson then cooked up the idea of bringing Free to the Coliseum via helicopter, Free popping out and walking up the red carpet for a press conference to announce his new contract.

"We needed something positive, something fun," said Weltman. "The fans wanted World back. We needed World. And we needed some good publicity."

The helicopter landing delivered exactly that. Free was a showman. He loved talking to the media, and they had a great time listening to him.

No matter how many times this was explained to Embry and others who dismissed Free's time with the Cavaliers as a strange sideshow, they refused to grasp the state of the game in Cleveland when Free arrived.

"I swear, they didn't even have all the lights on in the Coliseum during my first year," said Free.

World B. Free acknowledges a standing
ovation after scoring his 16,000th career
NBA point on Nov. 30, 1985 at the Coliseum.
Richard T. Conway / The Plain Dealer

That's a stretch. But basketball was in the dark ages in Cleveland until he began to light up the scoreboard.

*   *   *

My introduction to World B. Free was in the spring of 1974.

I didn't actually meet him. But I was with the Hiram College baseball team. We were on a spring trip and playing a few games at Guilford College near Greensboro, N.C.

We were sleeping near the gym. Many of the Hiram players had gone into town. It was night time. I heard a basketball bouncing. I went into the gym and saw a player shooting around. I loved pickup basketball. I walked over, talked to him for a while. His name was Billy Highsmith. He was a freshman on the basketball team.

This was the Guilford College basketball team that had won the 1973 NAIA national title. The Quakers—yes, that's their nickname—were led by a young man from New York named Lloyd Free.

Highsmith and I played a lot of 1-on-1 that night. He won every game. But he spent a lot of time practicing his jumpers rather than simply driving around me to make layups. He talked about Lloyd Free, how Free was going to play in the NBA.

I'd never heard of Free until that day.

Highsmith and I were playing in a shoebox of a gym. It was hard to imagine anyone from that small school and that tiny gym becoming a star in the NBA.

But Highsmith was right. Not only did Free play in the NBA, but so did his teammates M.L. Carr and Greg Jackson. Free was a second-round pick by Philadelphia in 1975. Carr and Jackson were future NBA fifth-round picks.

Highsmith would play four years at Guilford, averaging 10 points per game.

But the story didn't end there.

In the summer of 1977, I was hired to my first full-time newspaper job with the Greensboro News-Record. One of my assignments was covering small college basketball, which included Guilford. I met Jack Jensen, the basketball coach. He was an engaging man, a story-teller with a young reporter willing to listen.

He talked about going to Brooklyn to not only recruit Free, but Greg Jackson and others.

In the 1960s and 1970s, there were no AAU shoe-company sponsored summer tournaments for the nation's best high school players. They tended to stay near home. In the summer, they played on the playground, or perhaps in legendary settings such as the Rucker League in Harlem.

Free remembered playing against the asphalt legends such as

Phil "The Thrill" Sellers, who became a star at Rutgers. There was Earl "The Goat" Manigault, who could have been a star but battled drugs. He was revered on the New York playgrounds.

Free talked about Nate "Tiny" Archibald, another New York playground star who was terrific in the NBA. There also was Connie "The Hawk" Hawkins and so many others—virtually all with nicknames.

"So I had a nickname dating back to junior high," he said.

He was called "World," short for "All-World." He had a 44-inch vertical leap, whirling dunks and a global sized ego. Like many New York playground stars, he also talked lots of trash to opponents.

Jensen heard about Free and some others. Free was not exactly a star student. This also was a time when some major Southern schools didn't recruit black players, or at least were keeping an unofficial quota when it came to African-Americans on their roster.

The saying about how to use black players at some schools was "play one or two at home, three or four on the road . . . and five if you were in trouble of losing."

Jensen convinced Free to come to Guilford, and it was a place where he could play as many minorities as he wanted without worrying about public pressure.

Free didn't have a lot of other options. The same with Jackson, who teamed up with Free in the backcourt to win the 1973 NAIA title. Jackson would only play a single season in the NBA. He returned to Brooklyn and was well-known for his work with young people at the Brownsville Recreation Center, where Free played as a youngster.

I recently ran into Leonard Hamilton, the veteran coach from Florida State. He began his college career as an assistant at Austin Peay. We began talking about James "Fly" Williams, another playground star from Brooklyn and the Brownsville Recreation Center. Hamilton convinced Williams to come to the university in Clarksville, Tennessee.

Williams played there for two years, then turned pro.

But the point is college basketball was a much different place in the days of Lloyd Free. Those young men from the mean streets of New York and the small colleges in the South had to battle their way to the NBA. They weren't anointed "The Chosen One" as LeBron James was at the age of 17 when he appeared on the cover of Sports Illustrated. Shoe companies weren't recruiting young teenagers to attend camps that funnel them to the college basketball powers.

As Hamilton and Jensen told me, so much of the scouting was word of mouth. Someone knew someone who knew of a good player who needed a college.

"I know what it means to come from nothing," Free told me in 1986. "My father (Charles) was a longshoreman. His work wasn't steady. But the man always found something for us to eat. There were six of us and we lived in a one-bedroom place. We stuffed towels in the windows to keep the cold out. When my father worked, it went day-to-night-to-day. These long shifts. He'd come home and be about dead."

Basketball was Free's ticket. He shot his way out of New York to a small college in North Carolina. Then he shot his way into the NBA. And he kept shooting, kept scoring, kept talking.

"It started for me on the playground," said Free. "When I was a kid, Nate Archibald was the guy in Harlem. It was me in Brooklyn. Sometimes, I'd go there for games. Sometimes, he'd come to Brownsville. It was Nate the Skate vs. World the Thrill. It was like the Old West. Who was going to be the top gun? When we took the court, it was time to hook up your holsters, pull out your guns and see who could shoot each other's brains out."

Free told me that in 1986, it wasn't common for people to show up at playgrounds and start shooting with guns. He was talking about jump shots, dunks and layups. He was talking playground basketball as it once was, before AAU teams and shoe companies moved everything indoors and turned it corporate.

"I remember when I was one of those boys, sitting on the sideline, waiting to get into a game," he said. "I used to shoot left-handed. But no one shot left-handed, so I switched to the right hand."

Free could indeed shoot left-handed. After Cavs practices, he'd go to the foul line and make free throws with his left hand. His form was perfect. Then he'd practice his right-handed free throws.

His jump shot came from almost behind his head with a high arc.

"You learn that if you don't want it blocked," he said. "I learned that from some other guys on the playground."

He was cocky. He was relentless. He was a player and an entertainer.

"I didn't have the same advantages as a lot of guys," he said. "There was no big name school for me. No NCAA tournament. I had to make my way the hard way to the NBA."

Free said he has pictures of himself as a young player with the Sixers.

"I have my first pair of tennis shoes from the NBA," he said. "They are an old pair of canvas Converses, the Chuck Taylor model. I never knew who Chuck Taylor was, but I wore his shoes."

In the 1970s, few players had a shoe contract worth mentioning.

"People would take me to a fancy restaurant, and I'd order a cheeseburger and Budweiser," he said. "I remember being a rookie and going out to a place where they served oysters and lobster. What did I know about oysters and lobsters? How was I supposed to eat that? I asked the waiter to bring me some ketchup. The waiter looked at me and said, 'Sir, what did you say?' I told him to forget it. That was one of those embarrassing moments when I felt like I didn't belong with people with money. I felt so low, I could have walked out of the room without bothering to open the door."

*   *   *

I didn't cover Free and the Cavaliers until the 1985–86 season. But I saw games with Free.

"He was the only guy we had who the fans wanted to see in those years," said Joe Tait. "You had to be here to fully understand what World meant to this franchise. He was unfairly labeled, and too many people held things against him from when he was a younger player."

The World B. Free who showed up in Cleveland on the cold December day in 1982 was 29 years old. He was in his eighth NBA season. He made an All-Star team. The previous four years, he had been a 20-point scorer. In 1979–80, he averaged 30.2 points per game.

He was not a young, insecure second-round pick from small Guilford College outside of Greensboro, N.C., who joined the powerhouse Philadelphia 76ers.

He used to call himself "The Prince of Midair" because of his leaping ability. But that changed when he arrived in Cleveland at the age of 29. He was not the World who could dunk with ease. He was a polished pro, a jump shooter from long range with 3-point accuracy (.378 with the Cavs).

One of my first conversations with Free led to him asking, "Do you know how hard it is to get 20?"

"Twenty points?" I asked.

"No, 20 shots a game," he said.

I laughed.

Free was serious. He explained how defenses were set up to stop players like him, scorers on bad teams. The goal was to keep the ball out of his hands. And when he did have the ball, he often faced two defenders. It took strength, energy and ingenuity to get off 20 decent shots a game.

"It can wear you down knowing you have to carry the offense for your team," he said. "But I did it, year after year."

Critics of Free, such as Embry, ask, "What has World ever won?"

*　　*　　*

After three years with the Philadelphia 76ers, Free was traded from bad team to bad team. In his first full season as the starting shooting guard, those teams showed an average improvement of 15 victories.

"There was always an owner out there who knew I could help his team win," said Free. "Maybe he liked some other players better, but he knew World could bring their team alive."

It happened in San Diego, where the Clippers went from 27-55 to 43-39.

It happened in Golden State, where the Warriors went from 24-58 to 39-43.

It happened in Cleveland where the Cavs were 3-19 when he finally played and 20-40 after that.

In 1984–85, the Cavs started the season at 2-19 under rookie coach George Karl. He was trying to run a share-the-ball, passing game style offense. That was not going to work with a starting lineup of John Bagley, Roy Hinson, Phil Hubbard, Lonnie Shelton and Free. Those guys were more defensive-oriented players and not strong outside shooters—Free being the exception.

When Karl allowed Free to control the offense, the team began to win. The Cavs finished with a 36-46 record—34-27 once Karl turned Free loose. They made the playoffs and lost to Boston 3-1 in the best-of-5 first round series. Their three defeats were by a combined seven points.

Free averaged 26.3 points and 7.8 assists in the series against the Celtics, shooting .441 from the field.

He played well. The Cavs overachieved that season.

But the next year, GM Harry Weltman and coach George Karl went to war on a variety of fronts. Karl had two years left on his contract, but wanted a new deal as a reward for making the playoffs. Weltman did offer to change his contract a bit, but Karl wanted more.

In the 1985 draft, Weltman had a chance to pick Karl Malone. He had the future Hall of Famer in town for nearly two days. But right before the draft, Weltman instead selected Keith Lee. Karl dueled again with Free about playing more defense and having him share the ball more on offense.

It was a clash of egos.

I covered the team that year, my first on the NBA beat for the Akron Beacon Journal. Karl was 34 and immature as a coach. Free was 32 and had little respect for Karl. The two had played against each other in the late 1970s. Karl was a journeyman, a 6.5 point scorer in his career in the NBA and ABA. Free remembers having little problem scoring against the man who now was his coach.

By the end of the 1985–86 season, Karl and Weltman had been fired. The Cavs had drafted Ron Harper as shooting guard. Embry didn't believe Free would be content to come off the bench. His career with Cleveland ended at the age of 33—despite averaging 23.4 points and shooting .455 from the field (.420 on 3-pointers) in 1985–86.

He played two seasons after that with little success. It was almost as if the rejection by the Cavaliers broke his basketball heart. He is now a "basketball ambassador" for the Philadelphia 76ers, meeting with fans at games and other events.

He has often said Cleveland was the favorite time of his career. The attendance rose from 3,916 to 9,533 per game in his four seasons.

It's hard to explain World B. Free. You had to experience it. And Cavalier fans had the best version of Free from 1982 to 1986. In 275 games, he averaged 23 points, shooting .454 from the field.

"It drives me crazy when I hear people take shots at World," said Joe Tait. "Only those who followed the franchise back then understand what World meant to the team. His No. 21 should be hanging from the rafters. He was that good and that important to the Cavaliers."

Fans Write In . . .

The Richfield Coliseum

My memories of the Coliseum: The fun, hilly drive across Route 303 and the art of exiting the parking lot. And The Shot, thinking we had the game won after Craig Ehlo's layup, and the deafening silence walking out. (Editor's note: it was Game 5 of the 1989 NBA playoffs' first round; Chicago beat Cleveland 101-100 to win the series.)
—*Gregg Bollinger, Columbia City, Indiana*

I remember the bumper-to-bumper traffic as you were driving to the game. Driving a car with a stick shift was a real pain. I have had automatic cars since.
—*David Gibbs, Huber Heights, Ohio*

The Coliseum sold beer, but you'd never see anyone drunk or acting unruly at a game.
We saw countless games . . . "The Shot" by Michael Jordan . . . Jordan's 69 points . . . Craig Ehlo's game-winner vs. Utah ,,, knocking out Larry Bird and the Boston Celtics in 1992 . . . and many others. After the game, we always went to Whitey's on Brecksville Road, and you couldn't help but impersonate public address announcer Howie Chizek with every word you'd say. You'd methodically tell the waitress, "I'll have a cheeseburger with grilled onions and fries for THA-REEEE."
—*Mike Shaffer, Ashtabula, Ohio*

The orange-and-white uniforms of the '80s Cavs are my earliest memories, with John Bagley, Roy Hinson, World B. Free and my favorite, Edgar Jones. I think EJ created swag. He was the coolest, most stylized dribbler I've ever seen.

I asked my dad if we could go to a game at the Coliseum. The car ride through the forest on Route 303 was the farthest from urban sprawl that you could get. Out of nowhere, you'd see spotlights above the trees and then get to the giant parking lot. The Coliseum had vibe, energy and substance. I loved looking up in the rafters and seeing people walk around on metal bridges above the crowd and the court. It was just cool.

—*John Arakaki, Los Angeles, California*

One of my favorite memories would happen after the game. No matter how bad the Cavs got beat (and they usually did), my dad and I would go find the 8th Wonder of the World, Pete Franklin. He would broadcast his opinionated and brash talk show from a little plexiglass-wrapped studio in the outer concourse. Pete regularly declared, "I talk to more sports fans than anyone." He had the fan base to back up his self-aggrandizing persona. If we were patient, most fans would soon leave and we'd have a front-row view and could watch and listen. One evening someone rigged Pete's cigarette and it went off like a sparkler, creating a lot of laughs. I even managed to snag Campy Russell's autograph right there in the concourse.

—*Lonnie Raber, Landrum, South Carolina*

I went to the Coliseum with two buddies from high school. There was supposed to be one more, but he was in a car accident and still recovering. We got there early so we could get a note to Joe ("It's basketball time . . .") Tait. He always was wishing people happy birthday or get well during the pregame show. And he did wish our friend a speedy recovery on the air.

The Cavs were playing the Celtics and weren't expected to win. Good ol' Pete Franklin grabbed hold of the mic and got the crowd really fired up. He kept saying "Screw the Celtics!" louder and louder, and everyone was saying it with him. The Cavs ended up destroying the Celtics. Great night!

—*Dennis A. Durst, Marion, Ohio*

I can still hear the Coliseum horn. It was not an actual buzzer. It was like a 1970s Buick.

—*Neal Hausch, Akron, Ohio*

A friend was having a birthday party, probably his 9th or 10th, and invited me and several others to a Cavs game at the Coliseum. This had to be the Coliseum's first or second year. My friend's uncle turned out to be Cavs owner Nick Mileti, and our group watched the game from a loge. The entire group was given a poster, a color print of a Plain Dealer or Cleveland Press headline that read something like "20,250 see Cavs beat Knicks" or some other team. I probably stapled the poster to my bedroom wall and eventually threw it out. I wish I'd kept it.

—*Rick Gorski, Olmsted Falls, Ohio*

One of the great features of the Coliseum was the standing-room-only section at the top of the arena behind the last row. There was a wall to lean on and you could see the game fairly well. My dad on occasion would surprise me with tickets. My greatest memory is Game 1 of the 1992 playoffs vs. the New Jersey Nets. Drazen Petrovic lit it up for the Nets that night. The climactic point was Hot Rod Williams stealing the inbounds pass at the end of the game and breaking away for a dunk that sealed the victory.

—*Josh Hammond, Amherst, Ohio*

I had tickets to Game 7 of the 1992 Eastern Conference semifinals against the Boston Celtics. It was an afternoon game, and I decided to use the North entrance to the Coliseum. I remember seeing a crude cardboard sign hanging on a telephone pole with the words, "This Way to Larry's Last Game." Wow. In the fourth quarter, Larry Bird and Kevin McHale were sitting on the bench. The Cavs were holding on to a lead, and I expected both to enter the game at any time to try to shift the momentum to the Celtics. It never happened. The Cavs won and advanced to the Eastern finals. It was indeed Larry Bird's last game!

—*Mike Nowak, Cleveland Heights, Ohio*

When I was 15, I received two Cavs tickets for subscribing to some Cleveland sports magazine (I can't remember its name). It was for a February weeknight game. My friend's dad drove us to the Coliseum in a near blizzard and slept in the truck while my friend and I went to the game. There were maybe 3,000 there, but we got to see Pistol Pete Maravich play, which was pretty thrilling although he was toward the end of his career.

—Mike Kittelberger, Lakeland, Florida

We were in Richfield for The Shot by Michael Jordan. They had sold out the arena but put risers up behind the seats with folding chairs. We were in the last row of extra seats. I remember walking out after the game and my dad shaking his head and saying, "This is the best this team is going to be." He knew we couldn't get around Jordan.

—Dennis Sullivan, Ridgewood, New York

My son Pete and I attended games at the Coliseum when Mark Price was our favorite player. At one game, there were two men sitting several rows below us. One would say, "Do the right thing, Mutombo, do the right thing" to Dikembe Mutombo. Finally, he said, "Do the right thing, Mutombo, or I'm coming down there." His friend remarked, "You do and you're going alone." The fans around them roared with laughter, and when the men left before the end of the game, fans applauded in appreciation for the entertainment they had provided.

—Beverly Faust, Aurora, Ohio

I went to the Cavs' game with neighborhood friends on Dec. 30, 1975, vs. the Kansas City Kings. I purchased a program and got the lucky one with Coach Bill Fitch's autograph that allowed me to shoot free throws at halftime. I would have won a Cavs watch and everyone seated in my section would have gotten a free pizza. I remember going down to the court and walking past Nate Archibald and thinking how short he was. I had to make as many free throws as possible in 24 seconds. I was so nervous, I missed all my free throws—and so did my opponent. So we went into a sudden death overtime and I couldn't hit a

thing. I choked and my opponent made his. The announcer had said my name and section. As I dejectedly walked back, I didn't know there were high school friends from Lutheran East at the game. They came running toward me, screaming my name. I stopped feeling dejected. I don't even remember if the Cavs won. (Editor's note: They did, 110-106.)
  —*Dean Mahovlic, Westerville, Ohio*

My friend was confined to a wheelchair and had a car outfitted so he could drive and transport his chair on the roof. We would meet in Richfield and tour the concourse. It seemed like he knew everyone working at the Coliseum.
  I missed the Miracle in Richfield as I was in the Navy, but on Sunday, May 7, 1989, a neighbor called and said I was going to the Cavs-Bulls game because he had two tickets for me. My father had never seen a Cavs game in person. Of course we know what happened—Michael Jordan hung in the air for an eternity and nailed his shot over poor Craig Ehlo. The Coliseum went from delirium to dead silence. My father looked at me and we both just shook our heads in disbelief.
  —*George MacWherter, Cleveland, Ohio*

My favorite player was probably Foots Walker. I still have the Cleveland Press poster page of all the players on the Miracle of Richfield team. I would tape Joe Tait doing games, and studied those tapes all the time.
  —*Kevin Dawson, Trinity, Florida*

I grew up in Bucyrus and remember how the arena in Richfield seemed to be in the middle of nowhere. We went to a Cavs-Warriors game in the winter of '94 and my mom drove her rear-wheel drive 1985 Mustang. It snowed heavily while we were at the game. We couldn't find our car afterward. We waited until the arena cleared before we could see only a few cars left.
  —*Scott Davis, Arcanum, Ohio*

CHAPTER 14

The Wildest, Weirdest Cavs Draft

As I write this, I have a copy of the story in front of me,
    It was in the June 17, 1986, edition of the Akron Beacon Journal.
The headline reads: CAVALIERS DEAL HINSON TO 76ers FOR
RIGHTS TO DAUGHERTY.

Sounds like the typical headline on a news story. The Cavaliers
did indeed trade forward Roy Hinson to Philadelphia for the first
pick in the 1986 draft. And they did draft North Carolina center
Brad Daugherty with that selection.

Everything was factually correct. It happened exactly how I
wrote it for the Akron Beacon Journal.

Only I wrote it *before* it happened.

And I wrote it *as if* it had already happened.

And that fit in with a lot of strange things that happened on that
franchise-changing draft day.

Unlike now, the NBA draft was held early in the afternoon.

And unlike now, the Akron Beacon Journal was an afternoon
paper.

At this point, the Cavs had no coach, no general manager and
the team was being run by owner Gordon Gund, team legal counsel
Richard Watson and team president Thaxter Trafton.

There were two basketball people still in place: Barry Hecker
and Ed Gregory. Neither had much power.

I became friends with Trafton, who was in charge of the business side of the franchise. Early in his career, he did a little high school basketball coaching.

That was it.

Suddenly, he was the front man for the draft—at least to the media.

About 2 a.m. on June 17, the Cavs traded Hinson and $800,000 to Philadelphia for the top pick in the draft.

So that was a fact, already done, when Trafton and I spoke early in the morning the day of the draft.

"Are you going to pick Daugherty?" I asked.

"Yes," he said.

"I can write that?" I asked. "Our paper comes out early in the afternoon, right as the draft starts."

In NBA circles, there was a major debate about who was the best player in the 1986 draft—Maryland's Lenny Bias or Daugherty. So I had to be sure.

"It's Daugherty," Trafton said again.

"OK, I'd like to write the story like it already happened," I said.

Trafton agreed.

I interviewed him and quoted him as if the Cavs had already drafted Daugherty—even though they had yet to do so.

I quoted Trafton saying: "When you have a chance to get the best player in the draft, you have to go for it."

And Trafton also said: "In one sense, it's a gamble. Hinson is a fine person, a great player. The fans know and like him. But within a few hours, we got two 7-footers when (John) Williams' trial went his way and when we drafted Daugherty."

And Trafton explained: "People say we have too many big people. We feel you need as much size as possible. The league is getting bigger. Look at Ralph Sampson and Hakeem Olajuwon in the Finals. Young players can always be marketed . . . We'll make more moves."

In his first draft press conference as the team spokesman, Trafton was enjoying the moment with me on the phone—discussing the draft that had yet to happen.

I didn't have the name of the player the Cavs would take with the No. 8 pick. Trafton wasn't going to predict that, other than to say the Cavs liked Ron Harper. The shooting guard from Miami of Ohio was projected to go higher than No. 8.

Reading this story, I realize none of this would happen today. In 1986, there was no Internet. There are almost no afternoon daily newspapers. The story in 1986 was either in the morning Plain Dealer or the afternoon Beacon Journal.

And the Beacon Journal would become a morning paper in 1987.

I don't think I ever thanked Thaxter Trafton with as much gratefulness as he deserved for helping me out.

So Thaxter, thanks so much!

Trafton would leave the Cavs in 1987.

He had several good jobs after that, including running the Oakland-Alameda County Coliseum, the Arizona State Fair and something called the International Basketball League. He also would go into the Maine Sports Hall of Fame because of his talent as a high school basketball player.

*   *   *

Two months before the 1986 draft, general manager Harry Weltman was fired by the Cavaliers.

A week before the draft, interim coach Gene Littles quit. He knew he would not be around after the draft, and he had an offer to become an assistant coach with the Chicago Bulls.

At this point, the Cavaliers had no general manager in place.

Sort of.

Wayne Embry had verbally committed to be the Cavaliers' general manager, but he was still working for the Indiana Pacers as a consultant. In fact, he was in the Pacers draft room on the same day the Cavs were drafting players he wanted them to pick.

This would become a very awkward situation later that day.

Confusing?

That's the point.

No one knew what the Cavs would do because many in the NBA

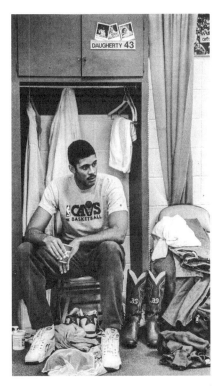

When the Cavs traded for the rights to pick
Brad Daugherty in the 1986 draft, it was a
gamble—for the team, and for the reporter
who reported the deal before it happened.
C.H. Pete Copeland / The Plain Dealer

doubted the Cavs had anyone in their draft room who knew what
he was doing.

But they had input from several places.

That started with Weltman, who was fired immediately after
returning from a scouting trip. He had no clue it was coming.
Weltman and former coach George Karl had engaged in a nasty
fight. Karl was unhappy about his contract. Weltman was unhappy
about some of Karl's coaching moves. Karl also had the desire to
have more influence on the roster.

Karl was fired with 15 games left in a season when the Cavs finished 29-53. His record was 25-42. Interim coach Gene Littles was 4-11.

Weltman's scouting reports remained with the Cavs after he departed. One name was at the top for the No. 8 pick—Ron Harper.

As far as I know, Weltman was not high on Daugherty. But he also wasn't scouting with the idea of the Cavs having the No. 1 pick.

When Gund, Watson and Trafton interviewed candidates to replace Weltman, they asked the men for their top players in the draft.

The final four candidates for the general manager's job were Rod Thorn, Rick Sund, Pete Babcock and Embry.

"We asked each of them to assess the draft for us," said Gund. "Out of that, a draft scenario began to emerge."

Embry soon became the favorite to be hired by the Cavs. He strongly favored Daugherty over Bias.

Embry had a lot of connections at Miami of Ohio, where Harper was a star. Miami was Embry's alma mater. Harper's coach for his first two seasons at Miami, Darrell Hedric, was a close friend of Embry. Hedric would later be hired by Embry as a scout for the Cavs.

Cavs fans knew about Harper, who played in the Mid-American Conference. Everyone wanted the athletic 6-foot-6 guard who left school as the leading scorer in MAC history.

When Harper was available at No. 8, the Cavs quickly called his name.

*   *   *

But what about the Daugherty deal?

That was the shocker.

Gund told me when he was at the draft lottery, he talked with Boston Celtics president Red Auerbach.

"It was before the lottery so no one knew where we'd be drafting," said Gund. "I asked who he'd take if he got the No. 1 pick. He said Daugherty."

In the lottery, Philadelphia won the top pick. Boston was No. 2. The Cavs had picks No. 8 and 29 in the first two rounds.

Gund said team attorney Watson was looking at the salary cap situation of every team.

"Dick was the key," said Gund. "He showed us how Philadelphia didn't have enough salary cap room to sign the No. 1 draft pick."

Now, that would not be an issue. This is the era of a rookie salary scale.

But in 1986, no rookie scale existed. Players sometimes held out. High picks often entered the NBA as one of the highest paid players on their teams.

"We knew even if Philadelphia wanted Daugherty, they couldn't sign him," said Gund. "We had a lot of room on our salary cap."

About 24 hours before the draft, Philadelphia was serious about trading the pick. Gund called Embry, who was going to be named the Cavs general manager a few days after the draft.

"I told Gordon if he could get the No. 1 pick, do it," said Embry. "I said to take Daugherty."

The Sixers and Cavs talked for hours. Philadelphia wanted Hinson, a 6-foot-9, 220-pound forward who'd just finished his third season with the Cavs. He was a good player, averaging 19.6 points and 7.8 rebounds.

But Philadelphia wanted more—Hinson and the No. 8 pick.

The Cavs also knew the Sixers had some money issues. And Gund's background was investment banking.

"How about Hinson and $500,000?" asked Gund.

That opened negotiations.

Philadelphia wanted $1 million and Hinson.

They settled on $800,000.

"Now, $800,000 doesn't like much," said Gund. "Back then, it was a lot of money."

Embry knew Philadelphia didn't want to draft Daugherty. The Sixers loved Hinson.

What the Sixers didn't know was that Hinson had a problem. He was only 25 years old but had painful knees.

Hinson had a good career, averaging 14.2 points and 6.8 rebounds. But it ended at the age of 29 due to bad knees. He went to work for the NBA Players Association.

Hinson was haunted by the trade in Philadelphia, where the fans were angry after Daugherty became an All-Star.

*   *   *

Remember how Red Auerbach told Gund that Daugherty was the best player in the draft?

Then the Celtics legend watched Gund trade ahead of him and draft Daugherty.

Auerbach took Len Bias with the No. 2 pick.

Most Cavs fans wanted Bias.

Boston fans were thrilled with the selection of the forward from Maryland.

At the press conference with the Boston media after drafting Bias, Auerbach had some interesting comments.

"Bias is the guy we wanted," he said. "I like him. Larry Bird likes him. He was the best athlete in the draft."

What about the Hinson/Daugherty deal?

"I'm not convinced it helped either team," Auerbach said.

Two days after the draft, Bias died of a cocaine overdose.

Just imagine if the Cavs had picked Bias instead?

Embry said he heard from Gund again the night of the Philadelphia trade. Gund said some people in the Cavs camp wanted Bias.

Embry begged Gund to take Daugherty, and that's what the owner did.

I've always wondered who wanted Bias. The Cavs had a scout named Ed Gregory, who had extensive experience as a college coach. He was the head coach at Fresno State and Nevada-Las Vegas.

The other was Barry Hecker, who was a high school coach before joining the Cavs in 1983 as an assistant to Weltman. Hecker also had been a small college coach.

Over the years, Hecker and Gregory have taken at least some

When Ron Harper was still available, the Cavs used the
number 8 pick in the draft to grab him. Here, in 1988, he
hugs Brad Daugherty after sinking a game-winning shot.
Nancy Stone / The Plain Dealer

credit for the 1986 draft. So has Embry. So did Gund, Watson and
Trafton.

But if the voice for Bias had ruled the room, it's doubtful anyone
would want their name attached to that draft.

*   *   *

The second round of the 1986 draft opened with Dallas on the
clock—and willing to trade the pick.

Embry was in the Indiana draft room, even though everyone

there from owner Herb Simon on down knew Embry was headed to Cleveland as the general manager.

Indiana wanted the Dallas pick—to draft Mark Price.

Cleveland wanted the Dallas pick—to draft Mark Price.

Suddenly, the market was hot for the 6-foot guard from Georgia Tech.

Rick Sund was the Dallas general manager. He had worked with Embry in Milwaukee. So the Pacers asked Embry to call Sund and make a deal for the pick.

Embry thought he had the deal done. The Pacers were thrilled.

Then Sund called Embry.

He explained the Cavaliers had been on the phone with Dallas president Norm Sonju, and Sonju took the Cavs offer.

"We gave them $100,000 and a second-round pick in 1989 for their (25th) pick," said Gund. "At the time, $100,000 was a lot of money. But we had already spent $800,000 for Daugherty, so we pressed on."

Indiana owner Herb Simon was furious when he heard Dallas had backed out of the deal—and traded the pick to the Cavs.

And the Cavs took Price.

Embry tried to explain he had nothing to do with the Cavs pursuing Price.

"I didn't even know the Cavs wanted Price," he said.

I tend to believe Embry. Before Price emerged as a star, Embry said his recommendations for the Cavs in the second round of that draft were Richmond forward Johnny Newman and California-Irvine forward Johnny Rogers.

Hecker and Gregory have both taken credit for drafting Price. That could be right, who really knows?

Trafton told me, "I saw Price on TV a few times and really liked him."

He said as much when Price's name was raised in the draft room.

Looking back, Indiana never should have had Embry in the draft room knowing he was leaving. And perhaps Embry should have stepped aside on draft day to avoid any conflict of interest.

"Indiana had the fourth pick," he said. "They were going to take (Auburn forward) Chuck Person. Cleveland was at No. 8. I didn't see a conflict."

The problem is things change quickly during a draft.

The Cavs acquired the No. 1 pick.

Then the Cavs were chasing the same second-round pick as Indiana, and both teams wanted Price.

History shows there is a Cavalier curse with many draft picks.

Just imagine if they had selected Bias instead of Daugherty. Or if the Cavs had waited just a little longer before trying to deal for the rights to Price—and he ended up in Indiana.

But in this draft, the Cavs were aggressive, wise and . . . more than a bit lucky.

CHAPTER 15

A Hot Rod With a Huge Heart

Perhaps the most memorable day of my writing career was spent in Sorrento, Louisiana.

The year was 1991, about 10 months after John "Hot Rod" Williams had signed a free agent offer sheet from the Miami Heat. It was matched by the Cleveland Cavaliers.

Compared to today's inflated NBA salaries, the 7-year, $26.5 million deal sounds very modest. But for the 1990–91 season, it paid him $4 million—the most of the any player in the NBA, including Michael Jordan.

This was during the time I covered the Cavaliers for the Akron Beacon Journal. I became close to Hot Rod and his agent, Mark Bartelstein. It's a long story dealing with Hot Rod being accused of point-shaving while playing college basketball for Tulane.

Former Cavs general manager Harry Weltman selected Williams in the second round of the 1985 draft while Hot Rod was still under indictment in the point-shaving case. Weltman investigated the case and believed Hot Rod was innocent.

So did Bartelstein, a young agent at the time with Hot Rod as his first client.

Both men challenged me to look into the case, which I did. It wasn't hard to see it was a sham. My sense was Hot Rod had been set up by jealous teammates who had received immunity to testify against him.

He eventually was found not guilty.

For a long time, I was the only media member in Northeast Ohio strongly in Hot Rod's corner.

That's why five years after the career-saving verdict, he invited my wife Roberta and me to his hometown of Sorrento. He wanted to show us the new houses he built—one for himself, one for the woman whom he considered to be his mother.

Hot Rod died in 2015 at the age of 53 from cancer. Remembering my trip to Sorrento, I looked back at some stories I wrote for the Beacon Journal along with my memory from that incredible June day spent with him.

Roberta and I flew to New Orleans, rented a car and drove about an hour to Sorrento. It was a one-stoplight town of 1,161 residents back in 1991. It was a town of trailers and alligators. It was 5 feet under sea level. Just outside of town, we spotted a couple of alligators sunning themselves near the side of the road. Huge blue and white herons fished in the small lakes and swamps surrounding the town. Hot Rod had built an 11,000-foot home.

He actually helped build it. Hot Rod also was a carpenter. He liked to draw up plans for houses.

"I have been doing carpenter work since I was 10 or 11," he said. "I had a friend named John Martin. He taught me. Together, we built the cabinets in my high school cafeteria. I built about 10 garages in town."

The house had six bedrooms, six bathrooms, a garage big enough for four cars. There also was a swimming pool with a waterfall, a game room, a tennis court and "a mud room."

I'd never heard the term before.

"It's the room where you first go into the house," said Hot Rod. "So me and the kids can go outside and play and get all dirty. Then we come in, get cleaned up before going into the house."

He also built two sinks in the bathrooms. A taller one for his 6-foot-11 frame, normal height for the rest of the family.

He also built a 3,000-foot home for his mother, Barbara Colar. She always wanted a big kitchen, so Hot Rod made sure she had a *huge* kitchen. We toured both houses—by far, the largest homes in Sorrento back then.

Hot Rod worked with a Fairlawn architect named Gerald Rembowski to bring his dream houses to life.

"All of this cost me about $2 million," he said. "That included an official NBA half-court with a 28-foot ceiling so I can go work out any time I want."

*   *   *

Then Hot Rod took us for a ride in his SUV, showing and telling the story of his early life.

He took us to a part of town where there were some small wooden houses up on stilts. The ground often oozes water in Sorrento.

He stopped at an empty lot.

"This is where Mama saved me," he said.

Then Hot Rod told the story of living in a small shack with a little porch that was falling apart. He lived there with his father, mother and a blind grandfather.

When he was 7 months old, his mother died. Not long after that, his father just left.

A neighbor lady heard Hot Rod crying on the front porch with the blind grandfather.

"She took me in," said Hot Rod. "We weren't any kin that I know of. My Mama just felt sorry for me. She was and will always be my Mama."

Barbara Colar worked as a janitor in an elementary school in the morning, then cooked at a seafood restaurant in the afternoon.

She named him "Hot Rod" because he loved to play on the floor with toy cars, making motor noises.

Hot Rod promised to take care of her once he made money as a basketball player. He said he was being paid by a booster at Tulane to play for the Green Wave and sent most of the money home to his mother.

Williams said his father showed up when he was 11 years old and

"The thing I'm most proud of in basketball was drafting John Williams," former Cavs GM Harry Weltman said. Few believed Williams' claims of innocence in the Tulane point-fixing case—until the jury found him not guilty. Here, "Hot Rod" listens to Cavs coach Lenny Wilkens in practice.
Richard Conway / The Plain Dealer

needed him to sign "some kind of paper." Hot Rod said he signed, then never saw the man again.

*   *   *

The next stop was a patch of sand surrounded by some pecan trees.

Hot Rod explained this was his first basketball court. He found an old bicycle rim, and took out all the spokes.

"Then I nailed it to a pecan tree," he said.

Someone gave him an old basketball with no real tread. That's where he learned to shoot. That made it even more dramatic to know that less than a mile away, Hot Rod had built his own NBA-style basket and half-court.

He then drove to a country store named R&B SuperWarket.

Someone had turned the letter M in market upside down on the sign.

"Coach Wall told the owner of the store if any of his players came to the store for food, he should give it to us," said Hot Rod. "Coach Wall said he'd pay for it."

Coach Wall was Tommy Wall, the local high school coach.

"He proved a lot of people wrong," said Hot Rod. "He came from a racist town. People said he couldn't coach black kids. About all of our team was black kids."

I remember Hot Rod fighting back some tears.

"I loved that man," he said.

Wall died at the age of 45 from leukemia. He never had the chance to see Hot Rod play in the NBA.

Hot Rod was upset that former Tulane coach Ned Fowler often took credit for his development into an elite college player.

"Not true," he said. "It was Coach Wall."

Then Hot Rod told the story of his high school—St. Amant—losing in the state finals.

"After the game, Coach Wall was crying," he said. "Not because he lost. He kept telling us how proud he was of us, and how people said he couldn't coach black kids. But we became a family."

Hot Rod paused.

"I miss that man," he said.

*　　　*　　　*

Not long after Hot Rod died, I received a call from Dale Brown. He was the legendary basketball coach at LSU when Hot Rod was coming out of high school in 1981. Brown had read my stories about Hot Rod's death on the Internet.

Brown told me how much he loved Hot Rod, knew him well. He praised Hot Rod for his work with kids in Sorrento and nearby communities.

"Coach," I said. "I always wondered. Didn't you recruit Hot Rod?"

"Of course," he said. "He was a big-time player, would have been great for us."

Brown said Hot Rod "lived in such a small trailer, you could barely fit three people in there. It was real poverty."

Brown explained that Hot Rod didn't have the grades and test scores to be immediately eligible to play for LSU. He would have had to sit out a year and pass enough courses to play the following season.

"But Tulane got him in and he played right away," I said.

"That's right," said Brown.

"Tulane is supposed to be a good academic school," I said. "How did that happen?"

"You tell me," he said.

We both knew the answer.

*   *   *

When Hot Rod was facing point-shaving charges, I got to know his lawyer—a veteran Chicago defense attorney named Mike Green.

He put me in touch with Tommy Wall, who was dying of cancer at the time.

Wall told me how he found a 6-foot-6 Hot Rod Williams walking in the hallway of St. Amant High. He convinced Hot Rod to come out for basketball.

"He said he couldn't play because he lived 5 miles from the school and had to work at a store after school to help his mother," Wall said.

Wall set up rides for Hot Rod to and from school. He talked to the store owner, convincing the man to let Hot Rod work on weekends. That way he could still bring in some money and play basketball.

Wall said Hot Rod "wasn't a great student, but he didn't skip class and hardly missed a day. He was a good kid. Teachers loved him."

Green and Wall told me of college recruiters stopping by Hot Rod's house and leaving some money so he could go to their college.

Tulane did more than that—$10,000 in a shoe box for Hot Rod and his mother.

Green told me Hot Rod ranked 181st out of a class of 262. He said an assistant coach from Tulane helped him to fill out the college application.

"Tulane brought him in without John ever taking the SAT," said Green. "Then they had him take it the first day he was there. His score was 450."

Green said the average Tulane student had a 1,100 SAT score. Somehow, the low test score was "fixed" and Hot Rod became immediately eligible to play.

"And Tulane was supposed to be the 'Harvard of the South,'" said Green. "They just used him. They were going into the Metro Conference and wanted a nationally ranked program. They were paying players. They were willing to do anything to win."

*   *   *

As the 1984–85 Tulane basketball season came to an end, Hot Rod was a projected first-round NBA draft pick. Some NBA teams rated him a top 10 selection.

But on March 26, 1985, Hot Rod was arrested on sports bribery charges for fixing games. So were two of his teammates. A Tulane student was arrested for setting up the fix.

The story becomes complicated. One of the players had a cocaine habit. He went to a drug dealer who then set him up with a student wanting to fix games. The players were given $18,000 (split several ways) to fix two games.

Two players were given immunity to testify, primarily against Williams. A third was given a plea bargain. The district attorney was Harry Connick Sr., father of singer Harry Connick Jr. He had higher political aspirations.

Connick set up Williams to be arrested, handcuffed and brought to the New Orleans Jail—where he had the media waiting to capture it all on tape. It was clear Connick saw this as a case where he'd receive a lot of positive media coverage—assuming he won.

Hot Rod was in deep trouble, at first believing the police were interested in NCAA violations. They kept asking him about how he got into Tulane, and was he paid to play there?

"I really didn't understand what was going on," Hot Rod once told me. "I needed help."

*　　*　　*

Mark Bartelstein is one of the most successful agents in sports. His agency is Priority Sports with about 50 NBA players and 80 players in the NFL. They also represent about 30 basketball players and coaches working overseas.

But in 1985, he was 25 years old and armed with an MBA from Northwestern. He and a man named Mark Just wanted to get into the agent business.

"We had a connection in Tulane who was trying to help Hot Rod," said Bartelstein. "He needed a good lawyer."

Just and Bartelstein became involved in the case. They hired Mark Green, a top Chicago-based defense attorney.

Green was astounded at the lack of evidence against his client—and angered by what he called "trial by ambush" to pin everything on Williams.

Williams admitted he was paid $400 after a game against Southern Mississippi, and $1,500 after a loss to Memphis State. Those supposedly were the two games that were fixed.

"I just thought they were paying me like normal," Hot Rod said.

He would find money in his dresser drawer about every week. Sometimes it was only $100, other times much more. It averaged about $400 a week in his senior year during the season, Williams testified at the point-shaving trial. He said it usually was delivered by a teammate, once in a while by an assistant coach.

Hot Rod went to trial. Before Green had a chance to even present the defense of his client, the judge declared a mistrial because the prosecutors failed to turn over evidence helpful to the defense. The judge also cited "misconduct and dirty tricks by the prosecution."

But Williams had to face a second trial. Green put Memphis State coach Dana Kirk and Southern Mississippi coach M.K. Turk on the stand. They watched tapes of their games (the ones supposedly fixed). They testified they saw nothing suspicious about how

Williams played against their teams. They didn't see it during the actual game, nor when they went back and studied the tapes.

Green pounded away on the players receiving immunity and/or soft sentences to testify against his client. He stressed the cocaine use by some players and students fixing the games.

Williams was never accused of drug use.

It took 2½ hours for the jury to come back with a not-guilty verdict.

*   *   *

Williams was picked in the second round of the 1985 draft by Cavs general manager Harry Weltman. The pick was criticized locally and nationally by many in the media. Williams also was originally portrayed as an "alleged" drug user and game fixer in some media accounts.

After his first trial ended in a mistrial, Williams thought he'd be able to play the 1985–86 season with the Cavs. But the NBA ruled against that, saying he had to await the result of the second trial.

That cost him the entire 1985–86 basketball season, and the $150,000 he would have been paid by the Cavs.

"We looked into the situation," said Bartelstein. "When I first met Hot Rod, he was such an innocent country kid from Sorrento. People were taking advantage of him. He was an easy target."

Bartelstein talked about Hot Rod "being scared" that no one would believe him. So much money was being passed around the Tulane basketball program, it was easy to assume some was for point-fixing.

"It was a brave thing for Harry Weltman and (Cavs owner) Gordon Gund to do when they drafted Hot Rod," said Bartelstein. "They believed in him when not many others did."

Weltman once told me: "The thing I'm most proud of in basketball was drafting John Williams."

Green is now an attorney in Hawaii. He likes to tell stories about Hot Rod, but his most poignant is his first meeting with his new client.

"When I first met him, he spoke slowly and explained what happened," said Green. "At the end, he had tears in his eyes."

Green also was fighting his emotions.

"Mister," said Williams. "Please help me. I didn't do anything wrong."

"You got a lawyer," said Green.

*   *   *

Williams had an excellent career with the Cavaliers, lasting nine seasons. His career stats were solid: 12.9 points, 7.1 rebounds, .482 shooting percentage and .730 from the foul line.

But the numbers didn't reflect his true value to the team.

At 6-foot-11, Hot Rod could play small forward, power forward and center. He was good enough to start, but often was the first substitute. Coach Lenny Wilkens loved to have a strong talent—a player good enough to start—coming off the bench.

"I used to tell Hot Rod and the other guys that it was more important who finished the games than who started," said Wilkens. "Hot Rod knew where every player was supposed to be on the court for every play."

And Williams was on the court when it meant the most.

Hot Rod loved Wilkens, calling him "Coach Lenny."

He blended in with Larry Nance, Brad Daugherty and so many others on the team. He was a quiet, unselfish, caring man.

"He didn't care about his stats," said Bartelstein. "He did things to make it easier for his teammates. He'd switch to help on defense. He moved the ball on offense. He set picks. He blocked shots. That's why Lenny loved him."

*   *   *

Williams retired in 1999. He spent every basketball off-season in Sorrento, then lived there full time after his NBA career.

"I was never going to run away from home," he said. "The people here knew me and they supported me (during the Tulane scandal). I never did anything to shame them."

Williams died in 2015 from cancer at the age of 53.

"I remember when Hot Rod played for us and lived in Copley (an Akron suburb)," said Joe Tait. "He had a lot of neighborhood kids over. He built a basketball court in his back yard and he'd go out and play with them."

Danny Ferry became close to Hot Rod.

"He was so humble," said Ferry. "He was close to people. He'd bring us over to his house in Copley during the season. He was a super teammate."

Hot Rod was active in his hometown's youth sports. He especially liked baseball. He contributed money to help build playgrounds and baseball diamonds.

"He lived in that big house until the very end," said Bartelstein. "People would drive by it, it was a local tourist attraction. He helped build other houses and a church. He was a small town kid who grew up but never changed—or forgot where he came from."

Bartelstein becomes emotional talking about his client . . . a client for life.

"I can't begin to explain the impact Hot Rod had on my career," he said. "We represent Steve Kerr because of Hot Rod. We represent Larry Nance Jr. because of Hot Rod. He changed my life and the lives of many others."

CHAPTER 16

Gordon and Joe and Seeing the Game

When Gordon Gund bought the Cavaliers in 1983, the first major decision he made after retaining general manager Harry Weltman was about Joe Tait.

"Gordon, we need to bring back Joe," said Weltman.

"That's a great idea," said Gund.

Tait had left the Cavaliers in 1981. One season of Ted Stepien and Bill Musselman drove him away from his adopted hometown and his favorite place to work. Tait worked for the New Jersey Nets in 1981–82 and then the Chicago Bulls in 1982–83.

In the summer, he was back in Cleveland doing the Indians games on television.

Tait was keeping an eye on the Cavalier situation. He had met Weltman a few times and believed sanity would return to the franchise, especially if Weltman was working for Gund.

Gund had never met Tait, but knew his work.

Gund lived in New Jersey, but he loved to listen to games on the radio.

"That was back when Joe was on 50,000-watt WWWE," said Gund. "You could hear him clearly at night. I loved his voice. When Joe Tait called a game, you could see the game."

That last sentence is so important.

Gund is blind. He lost his sight at age 30 to a disease called retinitis pigmentosa.

In 1989, I spent an afternoon with Gund in his Princeton, New Jersey, office. When I walked in, the room was not quite dark, but the light was very subdued. Gund explained that bright lights cause him to see a collage of colors in front of his eyes. They would just pop up, not taking any shape. It's why some blind people wear sunglasses inside.

"The colors can drive you crazy," said Gund.

He talked about how he began to lose his vision. Imagine seeing a full page in a book.

Then a half-page.

Then a few paragraphs.

Then a sentence.

Then a word.

Then a dot—a period.

That was the most distressing part of the disease. You don't go from being in the light into absolute darkness. You lose a little at a time. And you know what's gone is never coming back.

"Losing the ability to see people was the worst," said Gund.

He has been blind since 1970.

Gund learns by listening. He has assistants read news stories and business reports. He loves to listen to the news on radio and television.

But when it came to sports, Gund had a special set of eyes—those belonging to Joe Tait.

Gund absolutely wanted Tait back "to bring legitimacy to the franchise."

Tait "absolutely" wanted to be back with the Cavaliers. He used that word when Weltman called with the story of Gund's plans for the franchise.

From 1970–80, Tait had worked under the Mileti regime. He remains grateful to Mileti for giving him a start in major league radio with the Cavaliers and Indians. But he also knew Mileti was in a continual scramble for money.

Then came Stepien.

Then came what Tait considered working in exile. He was thank-

Despite his blindness, Cavs owner Gordon Gund could "see" the games thanks to Joe Tait's radio play-by-play and the roar of the crowd. *Brynne Shaw / The Plain Dealer*

ful for the jobs in Chicago and New Jersey, but Cleveland was his home by the early 1980s. He had turned down some network radio jobs because he didn't want to live in New York.

Gund and Tait immediately connected in their first meeting. Tait knew the Gund family was wealthy. He knew Gund was a brilliant businessman. All Tait had to do was hear a few details of how Gund came to own the Cavaliers and the Coliseum.

Meanwhile, Gund believed, "In the minds of the fans, Joe was associated with the good times of the franchise."

Gund understood the fans knew Tait would not submit to foolishness when it came to ownership of the Cavaliers. He proved it by leaving Cleveland in protest of Stepien.

Hiring Tait was a repudiation of the Stepien regime.

Gund also wanted legendary sports talk show host Pete Franklin doing his broadcasts from the Coliseum when the Cavaliers were at home. Fans knew Franklin also turned his back on Stepien as the two men engaged in a major feud. Stepien even sued WWWE because of criticism from Franklin. In the end, the station and the Cavs, in the summer of 1981, agreed to separate as part of the settlement.

Suddenly, the Cavaliers were on WBBG (1260-AM) from 1982 to 1984. It was a much weaker station than the 50,000-watt WWWE (now WTAM).

Gund had to sit through the 1983–84 season with the games on the station that was only 5,000 watts at night. By the 1984–85 season, the Cavs were back on "the Big One, the 50,000-Watt Monster" as Franklin called it. His voice boomed "over 38 states and half of Canada."

The power of radio . . . Gund understood that.

The power of respected voices—Tait & Franklin . . . Gund wanted them talking about his team.

Gund admitted there were times when Tait and Franklin "said things that made me cringe. When the Cavs were playing bad, you could tell right away in Joe's broadcast. He was so candid, so utterly unwavering."

But he also knew that's why they had credibility with the fans.

"Joe and Pete were the keys to us getting back the fans," said Gund. "People trusted them."

This was an age when ESPN was in its infancy. There was no Internet. The local radio and television stations combined with newspapers to deliver the stories of the day.

And there was something unique about radio when people heard that special voice. Tait and Franklin did more than speak to the head, they connected to the hearts of their fans. It was an intimate exchange. Fans often came up to Tait and Franklin talking to them as if they were old friends. Just as Gund began a close friendship with Tait in their first meeting.

It was the power of local radio in a certain time and certain place for fans of a certain age.

*   *   *

Late one night, I was talking to Gund from the office of the Akron Beacon Journal. We were having a background conversation about John Williams and the Tulane point-shaving case.

"Terry, I told you, this is background," Gund said.

"It is," I said.

"I hear you typing," he said.

"Gordon, I'm not typing," I said.

"Yes, you are," he said.

I looked around. About 10 feet from me, another reporter was typing on her computer.

"Gordon, there is another reporter a few desks away," I said. "She can't hear me, but you are hearing her typing."

Most people who have spent some time with Gund have stories about his remarkable hearing.

Tait talked about being in a meeting with Gund. There were about eight people around a conference table. Gund had them say hello. He looked right at them.

"He was memorizing where they sat," said Tait. "When he'd ask them a question, he'd stare right at them. He couldn't see them, but with his hearing he could sense where they were sitting."

When Gund sat down to eat, he'd feel the size of the plate. At banquets where Tait was present, he sat next to Joe. He asked Joe to tell him where the food was placed on the plate as if it were a clock—meat at 6 o'clock, peas at 3 o'clock.

Gund loved to imitate Tait.

"Left to right on the radio dial . . . "

"Wham with the right hand . . . "

"Wesley Person for THREE . . . GOT IT."

Gund wasn't sure why he developed an affinity for Person, who averaged 12 points in his five-year Cavalier career. A nice player, but nothing special.

It probably had to do with how dramatic Tait made Person's long 3-pointers sound on the radio.

*   *   *

The 80-year-old Gund is an amazing person.

He comes from great wealth. His father invented something called Kaffee Hag. We know it as decaffeinated coffee. His father later ran Cleveland Trust, which became Ameritrust.

Gund played mostly pickup basketball growing up. He did have some ability in hockey.

"I was captain of the junior varsity at Harvard," he said. "I was a defenseman. My main attribute was I liked contact."

When Gund graduated from Harvard, he went into the Navy. Then instead of going into his father's banking business in Cleveland, he headed to New York and started at the bottom of the financial world with Chase Manhattan Bank.

Gund was unpretentious even before his blindness. But after losing his sight, his compassion deepened. He drove hard business deals but stayed away from personal attacks. You can talk to people who were fired by Gund. Most like the man personally, even after they were dismissed.

They talk about him being a gentleman, a man with dignity and class.

He isn't mean or self-centered. He has a giving heart.

The Gund Foundation is known for its charity. Gund also has a foundation raising money for research of retinitis pigmentosa.

"The thing about blindness is it's living a loss every day," Gund said. "You hear someone say you should have seen a sunset or a flower. You can't see it. You find yourself walking into tables and chairs."

Gund doesn't say that seeking pity. It's a fact.

But it also makes him grateful for the relationships he has, and the memories.

He can still recall what the color blue looked like, or how basketball was played. That's why Tait would describe the colors of the various uniforms worn by the teams for the game. He would talk about features of certain arenas. He sometimes gave physical characteristics of star players.

During games when Gund would sit in the arena, he wore head-phones so he could listen to Tait's broadcast. Joe served as his eyes during the game.

I once asked Gund what he thought Tait looked like.

"I've never seen him," said Gund. "But I have a picture of Joe in my mind. He's a big man with a round face, at least that's how his voice sounds. I know he is kind of wide and stout, probably bigger than he wants to be. I sense a steady presence."

Gund was sad when Tait retired in the summer of 2011.

"No one did games like Joe Tait," he said.

CHAPTER 17

The Mouse that Roared

When the Cavaliers traded for the second-round draft rights to Mark Price, I compared him to Kyle Macy in the story I wrote about the team's 1986 draft.

And I meant the comparison as a compliment.

If you don't remember Kyle Macy, that's the point of my mentioning it. Macy was a sharp-shooting guard at Kentucky from 1977 to 1980. He played in the NBA for seven seasons with three different teams.

For his career, Macy averaged 9.5 points, shooting 50 percent from the field and 87 percent at the foul line.

It was a decent career for a rather slow-footed low first-round draft choice.

I put Price in the same box, the non-athletic, smart guard with a sweet jump shot.

I got part of that right. Price was a smart player.

And he became one of the best outside shooters in NBA history.

But like nearly everyone else who evaluated Price, I underestimated him.

Thirty-three years after the Cavaliers traded with Dallas for the 25th pick (top of the second round) in the 1986 draft, Price told me something I never knew about that draft day.

"I was really upset," he said.

"Because you were picked by Cleveland?" I asked.

"It had nothing to do with Cleveland," he said. "I had never been to Cleveland. I really had no opinion about the city."

"OK, so what was it?" I asked.

"I should have been a first round pick," he said.

"I see," I said.

"I really thought I was going to Atlanta (No. 19 pick)," said Price. "I would have fit in perfectly with that team with Dominique (Wilkins) and those guys."

Price was a four-year star at Georgia Tech, a four-year starter who made several All-America teams. He played right in front of the Hawks from 1982 to 1986.

What did the Hawks do with that 19th pick? They drafted a forward from Louisville named Billy Thompson. Then they traded Thompson and a player named Ron Kellogg to the L.A. Lakers for Mike McGee and Ken Barlow (23rd pick).

If those names mean nothing to you, that also is the point.

The NBA team that should have known Mark Price the best didn't really know the basketball player at all.

After Atlanta passed on Price, here were other players picked at the end of the first round: Buck Johnson, Anthony Jones, Scott Skiles and Arvydas Sabonis. Skiles had a good career. Sabonis was a star for the Soviet national team and played seven solid seasons in Portland.

But none of those players came close to matching the career of Price.

"In the long run, it worked out great for me," said Price. "I loved Cleveland. I still love Cleveland."

Price was relieved that someone called his name on draft day, even if he'd never spoken to anyone from the Cavs before the draft.

"I was totally in the dark," said Price. "It was first announced that Dallas picked me. I thought that was good. I'm from Oklahoma, and Dallas was not that far away. But then I got traded to Cleveland."

"What did you think about that?" I asked.

"All I knew was the Cavaliers had been so bad for so long," he said. "But then I thought about it. I wanted to be an NBA player. An NBA team had just drafted me. Here was my chance."

*   *   *

As I write this, I have the 1987–88 Cleveland Cavaliers media guide in front of me. The theme was three young players for the future.

The three players who'd just finished their rookie seasons and were pictured on the cover?

Brad Daugherty.

Ron Harper.

John "Hot Rod" Williams.

No Mark Price.

"That was after my rookie year," said Price. "I had a hard time. I was playing behind John Bagley. I had an appendix attack at mid-season. I had some other injuries."

Price averaged 6.9 points in 18 minutes a game that season. He shot .408 from the field, .329 on 3-pointers. Looked like another Kyle Macy.

"And right after that season, they took Kevin in the lottery," said Price.

He meant Kevin Johnson, a star point guard at California and the No. 7 overall pick in the 1987 draft.

"It looked like I was in trouble," said Price. "Bagley was still there, and he was the starter. You take a guy in the lottery, and figure he's supposed to start. Then there was me."

The Cavs traded Bagley to New Jersey a few weeks before the regular season started. But that still left Price and Johnson.

"I got into the best shape of my life for training camp," said Price. "And it helped me that Kevin missed a few weeks because of his contract situation."

In 1987, the NBA had no rookie salary cap slotting system. That meant rookies sometimes sat out training camp trying to secure lucrative deals.

"It worked in my favor," said Price. "I played a lot early in camp and got my confidence going."

Mark Price shoots during Cavs rookie camp in 1989. Larry Nance called him "Little Bit," because he seemed even smaller than his 6-foot height. It soon became obvious that he was a brilliant outside shooter—and much more. *Curt Chandler / The Plain Dealer*

I was covering the Cavaliers that season. It was when practices were open to the media. Price was brilliant. He was making shots from all over the court. His ball handling was much stronger than a year earlier. He seemed more poised, quicker.

"People talk about speed but they often have it wrong when it comes to basketball," Lenny Wilkens once told me.

Wilkens was a Hall of Fame point guard and the Cavs coach from 1986 to 1993. He was telling me why I'd misjudged Price.

"With a point guard, it isn't simply how fast he runs," said

Wilkens. "It's how fast is he with the ball. Watch Mark. He moves as fast when he's dribbling as when he's running (without the ball)."

Wilkens also explained about there being "straight line speed" and "basketball speed."

A track sprinter runs in a straight line. So much of basketball is the ability to move laterally, from side to side. It's a quick first step, a shrewd and sure change of direction.

Price had all of that. It's why he found ways to dribble between two defenders trying to stop him. It's called "splitting the double-team" because he seemed to slice them in half with a fake, a dribble, and a zip of a step.

In the 1987 training camp, it was obvious Price was so much more than a brilliant outside shooter.

He was on the road to becoming a big time point guard.

Meanwhile, Johnson showed up out of shape after his contract dispute. Price demolished him in most practices. He outplayed Johnson in the preseason games.

On opening night, Price was a starter for the first time in his NBA career.

"I give Wayne (Embry) and Lenny (Wilkens) a lot of credit," said Price. "They gave me a legitimate chance to win the spot. Then they stuck with me with and traded Kevin."

In the middle of that 1987–88 season, Johnson was traded to Phoenix as part of a huge deal bringing Larry Nance to Cleveland.

And Price was set up to become the best point guard in the history of the Cavaliers.

Seeing the improvement from Price's rookie year to his second season, Detroit's Isiah Thomas told me, "That little guy became the mouse that roared."

*   *   *

Price also had the benefit of Wilkens as his first NBA coach.

Price is the son of Denny Price, a former Phoenix Suns assistant who also coached in college at Oklahoma and Phillips University. Denny Price was much like Wilkens, a soft-spoken, brilliant teacher of the game who stressed the mental side of the sport.

Wilkens is not only in the Basketball Hall of Fame as a player, but also as a coach. He excelled in game preparation and adjustments during games. His degree from Providence was in economics. He loved tactics. Price saw the game in much the same fashion.

That's part of the reason Price developed so rapidly once given a chance to start. He had a coach who knew exactly how the young point guard should be employed.

Now, I'm going to call a timeout in this discussion to sound like a cranky old guy who said "the game was better back then."

Guess what?

When it came to young players being prepared for the NBA, the game was far superior in the 1980s compared with today. That's because most players entering the draft did so after at least three years of college.

Think of the three players (Williams, Harper, Daugherty) on the front of that 1987–88 Cavalier media guide, and let's add in Price. All of them played four years of college. Price was a 22-year-old rookie. They were much closer to being young men than the "kids" who enter the NBA now after one year of college. Most of them are teenagers. There is a huge difference in maturity between a 19-year-old and a 22-year-old. That's both mental and physical.

It's part of the reason Wilkens clicked with this team. They were all four-year college players. Price (Georgia Tech) and Daugherty (North Carolina) played in the high visibility, pressurized Atlantic Coast Conference. When the Cavs opened the 1986–87 season with three rookies in the lineup, the youngest were Daugherty (21) and Ron Harper (22) followed by Williams (24).

*   *   *

Price had a sensational career, better than Williams, Daugherty, Harper and Larry Nance. And that says a lot, because those players were terrific. Price, Daugherty and Nance have had their Cavalier numbers retired.

But other than LeBron James, I believe Price was the best player ever to wear a Cavalier uniform.

I know some fans will scream, "What about Kyrie Irving?"

Irving was more talented than Price. Irving hit the biggest shot in franchise history, the 3-pointer that proved to be the Game 7 winner in the 2016 NBA Finals.

In a game of 1-on-1 with Irving vs. Price with both players in their prime, Irving wins.

But Irving had a destructive streak when it came to team chemistry. It happened in Cleveland when he demanded a trade after reaching three consecutive NBA Finals. It happened in Boston after he left the Cavaliers, then bolted following two seasons with the Celtics.

A lot of Irving's teammates respected his talent, but many didn't enjoy playing with him. His mood swings, his blaming other players and ball domination made him few friends in the locker room.

He was at his best when playing with James, whose personality was strong enough to keep Irving at his best. But after three years, Irving wanted out of Cleveland and away from James, who was the best player in the world at the time.

What about Price?

Nance called him "Little Bit," because he seemed even smaller than his 6-foot height. Price handled the ball quite a bit, but he was very willing to be a part of the share-the-ball offense designed by Wilkens.

He was a brilliant outside shooter. He was a shrewd passer. His career .904 mark from the foul line is one of the highest in NBA history.

He was a .409 shooter from 3-point range in his nine seasons with the Cavs. He made four All-Star teams and was first-team All-NBA for the 1992–93 season.

From 1987 (when he became a starter) through the end of the 1991–92 season, the Cavs won 2-of-3 games with Price in the lineup. It was 1-of-3 when he was injured.

One of the biggest problems for the Cavaliers beyond finding a shooting guard after the trade of Ron Harper was their inability to find a decent backup point guard to Price. That finally changed in 1991 when they drafted Terrell Brandon.

Mark Price shakes hands with fans at the Coliseum in 1990 after speaking to a postgame crowd about his commitment to Christ. *Nancy Stone / The Plain Dealer*

"It was so much fun because we were building something," said Price. "Brad, Hot Rod, Ron Harper and myself all began our NBA careers at the same time (1986–87). Then we traded for Larry Nance the next season. The team had a real identity."

That's why I put Price ahead of Irving. He and the rest of the core group of Cavaliers from that era wanted to play for the Cavaliers.

"The fans immediately accepted us," said Price. "They gave us a real home court advantage."

The Cavs were a true team back then, not looking at their scoring averages. The fans sensed that togetherness.

"The last few years of my career weren't much fun because I had a hard time staying healthy," said Price.

In 1990, he suffered a major knee injury running into a scorer's table in Atlanta chasing a loose ball. He required ACL surgery.

He came back in 1991–92 to lead the Cavaliers to a 57-25 record and the Eastern Conference Finals. He made the All-Star team.

During the 1993–94 season, he broke his wrist in a game. The next year, he had a significant foot injury and played only seven games after being traded to Washington.

He also had several fingers broken, dealt with hip pointers and assorted bruises and pulled muscles.

*   *   *

As the Cavaliers declined after the 1994–95 season with Daugherty suffering a major back injury that eventually ended his career, trades were made to rebuild and add draft picks.

Price was shipped to Washington on Sept. 27, 1995, for a future first-rounder.

After leaving the Cavaliers, he spent a season each in Washington, Golden State and Orlando. He was not the same All-Star because the injuries wore down his slight 6-foot frame. Basketball also became a real business, "with all the moving around."

"We lived in Hudson and loved it," he said. "We went to The Chapel (in Akron), and that was very important to us."

Price has been an assistant coach or consultant with six different NBA teams since he retired.

Every time he walks into what is now Rocket Mortgage Field-House, he looks up and stares at his No. 25 hanging from the rafters.

"That means a lot to me, to have my number retired by the Cavaliers," he said. "I had a special relationship with the fans in Cleveland. I'll always treasure it."

Fans Write In . . .

Players

In 1970, when I was in the 4th grade, I had lunch with the Cavaliers. My father and I sat at a table with a very nervous person who had just been drafted. I think he was afraid he would have to speak to the crowd. I found out his name was Bobby Smith and he went to school at Tulsa. Another player at our table was Walt Wesley. When he stood up to leave, I asked him for his autograph as I was facing his kneecap. It was a great day, and my family has continued to enjoy the Cavaliers as season ticket holders since 1971.

—*Joel Zaas, Solon, Ohio*

When I worked for the Cavs as an intern in the early 2000s, I was asked to go upstairs to drop something off at Austin Carr's office. He was director of alumni relations then. I knocked timidly on the door and said, "Mr. Carr, I have an envelope for you." I went in, handed him the envelope and then became a blubbering idiot about how great he was and that it was a pleasure to meet him, etc. I asked if I could have a business card (mostly to show my friends that I met him) and his answer was the coolest phrase I have ever heard. He said, "My business card is up in the rafters, son," and then laughed his "hee-hee-hee" laugh. Epic.

—*Jeremy Edwards, Olmsted Township, Ohio*

When I was in high school, we would go to Valley Vista Park in Cuyahoga Falls during the summer and watch pickup basketball games. Apparently a lot of the Cavs lived down in the valley (west of Cuyahoga Falls and north of Akron) and would come and play at the park. There would be Craig Ehlo, Hot Rod Williams and Mark Price on occasion. They were laid-back and easy-going guys.

I worked at a college radio station and we would get to go to media day. I was amazed at the respect shown to us by Wayne Embry, Lenny Wilkens and the entire staff. They were a class organization. One of the guys I was with accidentally bumped into Cavs owner Gordon Gund on the elevator. My buddy apologized profusely to him, and his response was, "It's OK. I didn't see you either." (Editor's note: The Cavs' former owner is blind.)

Best memory ever.
—*Ted Davis, Akron, Ohio*

I met Craig Ehlo at a Chevy dealership in Cuyahoga Falls. He signed my basketball card on both sides. At 8 years old, I remember thinking that was pretty special. Both sides. I remember him laughing about how the card was a shot of him going up for a rebound and essentially just a picture of his armpit.
—*Dennis Sullivan, Ridgewood, New York*

My favorite player was Mark Price, still one of the best shooters I have ever seen. Following the 1991–92 Cavs got me through a yearlong military overseas deployment.
—*Christopher Urban, Tucson, Arizona*

I remember loving Edgar Jones (The Count), of all people. Roy Hinson and Mel Turpin were fun to watch. In one game, Turpin got the ball in traffic, close to the rim, and just went right up and dunked on some unsuspecting player. We were all like, "Dinner Bell Mel!"
—*Frank Pangas, Fairlawn, Ohio*

I saw Mark Price during an off-season at a paint store. He came in with probably more paint on him than on the project back home. He mumbled something about a "honey-do" list. He was the one painting, not a contractor.

Bill Laimbeer and his wife lived in a condo just around the corner. I marveled at his size-15 shoes, wondering where he could find them, but he assured me that as long as he wore "tennis shoes," he received a new pair every week. His car was a Honda Civic, the smallest Honda on the road at that time, with the front driver's seat removed. Bill would drive from the back seat. When he was driving by, all you would see were his knees and arms. He was a warm, friendly sort—not the reputation he developed on the court for the Detroit Pistons.

—*Bob Woodruff, Sagamore Hills, Ohio*

I went to the Cavaliers' premiere game and many others at the old Arena. Bobby "Bingo" Smith was my favorite player. He had a beautiful jump shot and was never afraid to take a big shot. I had a chance to play with him in some pickup games at Cleveland State in the summers of 1972 and '73.

—*Tim Corbett, Ladera Ranch, California*

I remember going to a game and afterward staying for a concert that Mark Price put on with his singing group, Lifeline. I got a signed poster and I hung it in my basement, where my brother and I would play with a Nerf basketball hoop set. I shared this story on my radio show in Columbus and tweeted the audio to Price. I felt like a kid all over again when he responded with encouragement for me to "keep shining" my light for God.

—*Josh Hooper, Columbus, Ohio*

I met World B. Free once after a game. It was at a 7-Eleven, and the Cavs had lost after a John Bagley last-second shot would have won the game. World walked into the convenience store in a full-length fur coat and purchased an adult beverage. As he walked by, I asked him what he thought of Bagley's shot. He looked me in the eye and said, "I think I should have took it." That was World B. Free!

—*Patrick Schell, Lewis Center, Ohio*

I consider the lowest point in the Mark Price/Brad Daugherty era to be the trade of Ron Harper. About eight of us were in a dorm room at

Cleveland State listening to the local sports show. We were absolutely devastated! None of us could come up with a positive outlook about the deal. As it turned out, the off-court concerns about Harper were unfounded. What a sad day. I'm as burned up about it today as I was that night. He was my favorite player.

—*Greg Abbate, Surprise, Arizona*

I rode with Mark Price at a Cavs golf outing at Tanglewood Country Club in the early 1990s. After shanking one of his tee shots, he exclaimed, "Shoot (probably the worst curse word that he ever uttered). I do not understand how the pro golfers hit them so straight." Then, in a humble manner, he chuckled and said, "But they probably don't understand how I hit 90 percent of my foul shots."

—*Bob Paulson, Chagrin Falls, Ohio*

I was 12 years old and met Jim Chones and Foots Walker in 1974 at the New Market Mall in Painesville. My parents were wondering who the really tall guy was. No one went up to ask them for an autograph. My parents coaxed me. Neither of them had a pen. My mom gave me a pen. Chones had to show Walker, a rookie, how to sign autographs.

—*Drew Cate, Tallmadge, Ohio*

In 1992, I was a senior in college at Brandeis University in Waltham, Mass., (where the Celtics practice). I was walking into the gym in my Cavs T-shirt when a bus pulled up and out stepped Brad Daugherty, Mark Price and Lenny Wilkens and all the Cavs. They were practicing for a game at the Boston Garden that night. I told Lenny that I was from Cleveland, and he said, "Let's give this Cleveland guy a hug!" And Daugherty gave me a big bear hug and they let me stay and watch practice. Best Cavs meeting ever.

—*Jonathan Leiken, Shaker Heights, Ohio*

Did you ever wonder what it would be like to go 1-on-1 with an NBA player? I came close in about 1990. Four of us from our Bedford industrial league signed up for Hoop-It-Up, a national 3-on-3 tournament that went from city to city. We were in our mid- to late-30s and felt we had the skills and conditioning to go far. We ended up in the "Older Than Dirt" division and easily disposed of our first opponent. Then we drew a team of retired, older and somewhat out-of-shape ex-Cavs— Austin Carr, Bingo Smith, Barry Clemens and Tom Chestnut.

We started off strong (I even scored over Bingo, and he swore he was trying), but at some point I realized we were just being toyed with. Those guys began to put on a clinic, dropping 3-pointers and scoring at ease down low. We ended up losing by double digits. We had played as a team for years, but they were just thrown together for this tournament. I could only imagine the amazing skill level they had in their prime.

—*Bob Frankish, Macedonia, Ohio*

I've been a Cavs fan since I was in high school at Medina High from 1970 to 1973. My dad took me to see the Cavs play Portland as my Christmas present in 1971 at the Cleveland Arena. I was able to attend games at all three arenas.

I was Joe Tait's sound engineer on the morning news at WJW-AM and spent two or three seasons as audio technician at WWWE-AM for Cavs broadcasts. There were a few occasions when I was invited to work with the inimitable Pete Franklin in the studio. He was a sweet, generous man—who occasionally threw things.

—*Valerie Cooper, Providence, Rhode Island*

I was lucky enough to attend Austin Carr's basketball camps in the late 1970s, at Gilmour Academy and John Carroll University. AC actually participated in running the camps. It was not unheard of to meet him. Some of us caught a ride one night in his BMW from the gym to the dorms and got to hang out with his brother and future NBA player Scott Roth, who were counselors. It was cool for a 12- or 13-year-old.

Bingo Smith came one day and worked with the campers. They had a bunch of us get into a defensive position and hold it. Being picked as the kid with the best defensive position was a thrill for me, and I got to shake hands with the two Cavs legends.

—*Rick Solomon, Beachwood, Ohio*

In 1986, Brad Daugherty and Keith Lee came to Brunswick High School to give a talk about education. A few students kept asking questions about Mel Turpin and his weight issues. Both players would try to be professional and say things like, "That's something he's working hard on." You could see, though, they were trying not to smile. Finally, one student asked if the players called Turpin "Dinner Bell Mel." Daugherty and Lee couldn't take it anymore. They exploded in laughter.

—*Mike Shaffer, Ashtabula, Ohio*

In the early 1990s, I was sitting at Covenant Church in Hudson. A tall gentleman had to duck to make it through the sanctuary doors and sat next to Cavs assistant coach Dick Helm, who attended services regularly. My dad whispered, "That's Brad Daugherty." He didn't need to tell me. After being dismissed to Sunday School, I excitedly told everyone. The second we were dismissed from class, I sprinted back upstairs, tracked down Brad and had him autograph my church bulletin (which I still have, 27 years later). The pastor later sat me down and told me not to ask for autographs again.

—*Joel Voorman, Canton, Ohio*

I was at our church, The Chapel, in Akron on a Sunday and a few rows down from my parents was a familiar-looking man. I kept trying to figure out who he was and how I knew him. All of a sudden, it hit me. It's Craig Ehlo! It was cool to see someone "famous" hanging out at the same church I went to. During that era, several team members would occasionally come to the church. It made them seem relatable.

—*Dennis A. Durst, Marion, Ohio*

CHAPTER 18

A Game from 1988

Remote in hand, I was clicking across the channels when I saw . . . *me*, on TV.

It was me, back when I was too dumb to know no matter how long you grow hair on the side of your head, you're still bald on top. It appeared I was auditioning for a Ben Franklin look-alike contest.

Yikes! That was embarrassing.

But there I was covering a Cavaliers game when the NBA was a different place. It was when the Cavalier beat writers were assigned to sit at the scorers' table, right next to the Cleveland bench.

This was a Cavaliers/Chicago Bulls game from March 25, 1988, being broadcast as part of the NBA TV channel's "Hardwood Classics" series.

This was not Michael Jordan's "Shot" in Game 5 of the 1989 playoffs. It wasn't a playoff game at all. It was just a March night in the NBA from decades ago at my favorite place to watch a game . . .

The Richfield Coliseum.

As I tuned into the game, the camera zoomed into the Cavaliers huddle. Coach Lenny Wilkens was drawing up a play. I saw my bald head staring into the huddle, watching Wilkens scribbling his Xs and Os on a white board.

The Cavs came out of the huddle onto the court . . .

Mark Price.

Ron Harper.

Larry Nance.

Phil Hubbard.

Brad Daugherty.

That was the Cavs starting lineup that night. I found the game as the second half began. The Cavs were losing.

The television coverage featured the Chicago Bulls broadcasters, Jimmy Durham and Johnny Kerr. They kept talking about how Cleveland and the Bulls "were the NBA's teams of the future." They praised general manager Wayne Embry for putting together the Cavs roster. They talked about Lenny Wilkens being the right coach for this young team.

The Bulls were coached by Doug Collins. They praised him as the ideal coach for Jordan. It took a couple of minutes for me to realize the tall guy next to Collins was Phil Jackson, an assistant coach. Jackson was clean-shaven, imported from the Albany Patroons of the minor league Continental Basketball Association (CBA) by Bulls general manager Jerry Krause. Jackson was there to help Collins. He also was Krause's choice to take over for Collins if the Bulls didn't progress as the general manager expected.

That would happen a year later.

The Bulls starting lineup ...

Michael Jordan.

Charles Oakley.

Brad Sellers.

Sam Vincent.

Dave Corzine.

This game was so long ago and the Bulls were so young, future stars Scottie Pippen and Horace Grant were coming off the bench.

And the Cavs?

They had John Williams, Craig Ehlo and Dell Curry coming off their bench.

These were two good teams who indeed would be battling it out in the playoffs for several years.

*   *   *

As I write this, I can close my eyes and not only see the Coliseum, I can feel it shaking . . .

I can hear the crowd of 19,876 screaming . . .

Over and over, they chanted: "LET'S GO CAVS . . . LET'S GO CAVS."

Or: "DEE-FENSE . . . DEE-FENSE!"

The Coliseum had a nice overhead scoreboard, not a Humungotron like the monstrosity that hovers over the court at Cleveland's Rocket Mortgage FieldHouse today. This was before the Internet, cellphones and the obsession with e-sports and video games. The scoreboard supplied basic information, and maybe a few commercial messages.

The fans were there to be entertained by the game, to feel the energy from the court and their cheers from the seats. It also helped that the "luxury boxes" at the old Coliseum were up near the ceiling. That allowed "regular fans" to sit much closer to the court—where they could be heard. In 1988, fans didn't have to take out a second mortgage to be near the floor. Prime seats in the lower bowl went for $18 each.

Those same tickets for an average game in the 2018–19 season were $95.

Here is the disclaimer: Every sports fan has a sense of nostalgia for the era when they fell in love with their favorite team.

The Cavaliers of the late 1980s-early 1990s were my favorite team.

And the spring of 1988 was a special time.

Hope.

That's what this team represented to the Cavalier fans.

*　　*　　*

Watching the game that was played more than 30 years ago, I kept thinking, "Everyone looks so young!"

Neither team had a clue what was coming. At this point, the NBA was ruled by the Los Angeles Lakers, the Boston Celtics and the emerging Detroit Pistons.

The Bulls were trying to build a roster around Jordan.

The Cavs were trying to construct a team with no superstar, but a group of high-character, unselfish and very talented players.

Six-foot Mark Price looked like he was a senior in high school, not a 24-year-old in his second pro season. I watched him dribble the ball up the court. As he reached the top of the key, Brad Daugherty came from under the basket to set a pick.

The 7-foot Daugherty was only 22 years old and had the face of a high school sophomore.

As Daugherty set a pick on Price's man (Chicago's Sam Vincent), Price took a dribble, then stopped at the foul line. For a brief second, it appeared Price would take a jumper.

But Daugherty was lumbering to the rim. His man (Chicago's Dave Corzine) had stopped to stare at Price. And Daugherty was wide open. Price delivered a perfect pass.

Daugherty layup . . . two points for Cleveland.

Chicago broadcaster Johnny Kerr was a former NBA center. He raved about Daugherty's ability to set picks, catch passes on the move and score with fluid grace near the rim.

"Fundamental basketball!" marveled Kerr.

That was the Cavs in their second season under Wilkens.

The ball moved from side-to-side of the court. Players created "spacing," meaning they were not standing in the same area.

The ball moved . . .

The players moved . . .

The passing was crisp, often leading to open shots . . .

It was basketball the way it was supposed to be played—or at least, the way those of us of a certain age thought it should be played.

Daugherty would set his 260-pound frame near the basket in the low post. And the Cavs knew how to pass him the ball in that spot.

Why?

Because Wilkens had his players do it over and over again in practice. He showed them the proper angles to pass to a big man close to the rim. He showed the big man how to position his body to keep his defender on his back and create an excellent target for

Brad Daugherty and Cavs head coach Lenny Wilkens. *Richard T. Conway / The Plain Dealer*

the passer.

How do I know this?

Because this was an era when the media was allowed to watch practice.

As Danny Ferry told me, "Lenny had a beautiful offense."

It was refreshing to see teams not obsessed with the 3-point shot. They believed an open 15-footer was a good shot. Today's analytics insist a 25-footer for three points is better than a 15-footer for two points. The best modern offenses are supposed to feature 3-point shots or drives to the rim resulting in layups and/or dunks.

Nothing in-between. Long or short shots, period.

Wilkens wanted his team to take smart, uncontested shots within a reasonable distance of the basket.

In this game, the Bulls were 2-of-3 on 3-pointers. Wilkens liked the wide open 3-pointer for certain players. The Cavs were 3-for-8.

Chicago's offense was often stagnant. The Bulls often allowed Jordan to take the ball at the top of the key and create his own shot while the other four players watched. At times, Jordan would dribble and dribble and dribble, often drawing a double-team on defense. With the 24-second clock ticking down, he'd fire a pass to John Paxson or Oakley for an open jumper.

This isolation offense would eventually lead to Collins being fired and replaced by Jackson, who installed a "triangle" offense. It was different from what Wilkens employed, but it created the same ball and player movement.

Watching Jordan against the Cavs in the late 1980s—and the contrasting offenses—led Krause to make the coaching change. The general manager believed his team would never win a title with the "All Michael, All The Time" offense. And he didn't trust Collins to make the changes he wanted.

*   *   *

I covered the game, but have no memory of it.

I still don't know why NBA TV featured it 31 years later. It had no significance in the standings. Jordan finished with 39 points. That's a lot. But not 50 or even 60 points as he sometimes scored against the Cavs. In that 1987–88 season, Jordan averaged 35 points.

So his 39 points on 14-of-29 shooting wasn't anything special.

The Bulls won, 111-110, in overtime. But there was no buzzer-beating shot by Jordan.

The Cavs had an impressive shot-blocking defense. In one sequence, John Williams swatted away a Jordan layup. Oakley grabbed the ball, tried his own layup—and Williams blocked that, too. He had four blocks in that game.

Nance scored 29 points and had 11 rebounds and six blocks. He played so cool and with so much poise.

But the Cavs were crushed on the boards, 60-33. Chicago often dominated the rebounding when facing the Cavs. Part of it was Nance and Williams leaving their men to try to block shots, especially on Jordan. That created open lanes to the rim for the Bulls' big men to grab offensive rebounds.

Looking back, it was a fascinating game in terms of what was to happen in the next few years.

Here were the four Cleveland guards who played in that game: Ron Harper, Craig Ehlo, Mark Price and Dell Curry.

Curry is the most interesting of the group because it's easy to forget the Cavs once had him. In 1986–87, Curry was a rookie who played little for Utah. In training camp, the Cavs traded Mel Turpin to Utah for Kent Benson and the 6-foot-4 Curry.

Embry loved Curry for his outside shooting. In his one season with the Cavs, Curry averaged 10 points per game in 19 minutes. He shot 46 percent from the field coming off the bench.

When that season ended, Charlotte was entering the NBA as an expansion team. Each established team was allowed to protect eight players.

The Cavs' final decision for the list came down to Curry or small forward Mike Sanders.

In this March 25 game against the Bulls, Curry came off the bench sizzling, scoring 24 points on 10-of-20 shooting. Sanders played eight scoreless minutes.

By the end of the season, Sanders was playing a lot as a small forward whose main job was defense. Sanders was 27 and it was clear he was a hustling player with limited physical ability. There always are a number of players like Sanders floating around the NBA in any given season.

But there are few who shot the ball as well as Curry, now or in the late 1980s. Curry also was only in his second NBA season.

I recall a conversation with Embry when I said, "I assume you are protecting Curry."

There was a long silence.

"Wayne," I said. "Who else?"

He said Wilkens liked Sanders.

"Wayne, Charlotte is not going to take Sanders. You have to know that. But if you leave Curry exposed, any expansion team would take him."

Embry didn't want to discuss it.

Sanders was protected. Curry went to Charlotte. Curry played

16 NBA seasons, averaging 11.7 points. As the 3-point shot became more popular, his value increased. He shot 40 percent behind the arc. His son, Stephen Curry, has become one of the greatest 3-point shooters in history. Stephen Curry was born in an Akron hospital during the one season his father spent playing for the Cavs.

A little over a year later, the Cavs traded Harper to the L.A. Clippers.

Suppose they had protected Curry. Suppose they had Curry and Ehlo to fill in for the departed Harper, instead of only Ehlo.

The Cavs went from a tall, talented group of shooting guards (Ehlo, Harper and Curry) all in the 6-4 to 6-6 range to only Ehlo less than two seasons later.

But on March 25, 1988, no one knew Jordan would go on to win six titles . . . and the Cavs none.

No one knew Curry and Harper would soon be gone.

No one knew the Cavs would face Jordan five times in the playoffs . . . and never win a series.

No one knew Chicago was destined to be great, while the Cavs and their fans would be frustrated with simply being good.

But this much I did know back then—and still do when thinking about the game more than three decades later.

That was a special time in Cavs history.

CHAPTER 19

The Agent from Cleveland

Until Mark Termini told me the story, I'd forgotten about men holding up what looked like ping-pong paddles at the scorer's table of the old Cleveland Arena.

This was in the late 1960s when the Cincinnati Royals played some regular season games in Cleveland. It was before the days of huge scoreboards. It was when the 24-second clock was a little box-type thing on the edge of the court under each basket.

And when a foul was called, a man at the scorer's table would hold up two paddles—each with a number.

The first paddle revealed how many personal fouls were on the player.

The second paddle gave the number of team fouls for the period.

Termini was at Holy Name Elementary School when he went to the old Arena with his father, Marlo Termini. Older high school basketball fans may recall Marlo as a coach at Cleveland area schools Holy Name, Glenville, Benedictine and Walsh Jesuit. He also was an assistant coach at Cleveland State University. Like many coaches/teachers of his era, Marlo Termini had part-time jobs.

One of them was working at the scorer's table at the old Arena during Royals games. After the games, he also delivered copies of the box scores to the locker rooms. His young son Mark would tag along.

"I remember seeing Jerry West after a game putting hair spray on and styling his hair, which I thought was very cool," said Termini. "And many years later, I was negotiating NBA contracts with him."

That's because West went from a Hall of Fame guard with the Los Angeles Lakers to an NBA general manager.

And Termini went from the son of a part-time stats man and high school coach to one of the NBA's most prominent agents and attorneys.

*   *   *

I first met Termini when we were both in junior high at Catholic schools. He was a very good basketball player for Holy Name. I was a very bad one for St. Barnabas in Northfield. I was aware of him because my father (Tom Pluto) knew Marlo Termini. My father talked about how that "little kid Termini" could really play. Marlo was a star high school basketball player at 5-foot-3. His son Mark is about 5-foot-7. The son went on to average about 20 points a game for Case Western Reserve University.

When Mark was doing that, I was attending Cleveland State and working part-time at the old Cleveland Press. One of the stories I wrote was about Holy Name basketball, where Marlo Termini was the coach. One of the team's best players was Mel Termini, Mark's younger brother.

Many Cleveland basketball fans may not know about Mark Termini, but they probably have heard of Rich Paul.

Paul is a Benedictine graduate and the agent for LeBron James and many other NBA stars. But the man who actually structures and primarily negotiates the contracts for the agency known as Klutch Sports Group is Termini, who has a law degree from Cleveland State's Cleveland-Marshall College of Law.

Termini and Paul joined forces in 2012. Paul approached Termini and asked him to run the contract negotiations for his new Klutch Sports Group agency, then based in Cleveland. It's a unique combination. Termini negotiated his first NBA contracts in 1986, when Paul was entering the first grade. So Klutch is a mix of old- and

Long before Mark Termini became a top sports agent, he sometimes tagged along when his father worked at the scorer's table in the old Cleveland Arena. *Dale Omori / The Plain Dealer*

new-school agents.

Their client list includes John Wall, Ben Simmons, Draymond Green, Anthony Davis, Tristan Thompson, Darius Garland, Jordan Clarkson and James. They have negotiated close to $1.5 billion worth of contracts since 2014.

The Paul/Termini combination is one of the most influential in the NBA, and it's two guys from Cleveland.

*   *   *

I first talked business with Termini in 1986. He had just entered the sports agent world a year before, but now he was representing two top NBA clients—Brad Sellers and Ron Harper.

Both were first-round picks in the 1986 draft.

This was before there was a rookie salary scale. First round picks sometimes missed part of training camp until a deal was worked out. I was covering the Cavaliers for the Akron Beacon Journal. I spent time talking to Termini to find out when Harper would sign. After a three-week impasse, he did. Harper did not miss any games.

Talking about Harper began not only a business relationship but a long-time friendship.

Yet I never asked Termini how he became an agent.

Because of his father and his own basketball connections as a good Cleveland area high school and college player, Termini had relationships that paid off.

He was friends with a high school player named Phil Saunders. That's the same "Flip" Saunders who was a star at Cuyahoga Heights High and then played in the Big Ten for Minnesota.

In 1977, Saunders became the head coach at Golden Valley Lutheran Junior College in Minnesota. After his first two seasons, he hired Termini as his assistant.

"I'm not sure how much Flip really wanted me for the coaching," said Termini. "I helped him recruit a very good player from Glenville named Nelson Johnson. I'm pretty sure he was more interested in Nelson than me."

Termini smiled as he told the story.

That's because Termini and Saunders would remain very close friends for 43 years, until Saunders died of cancer in 2015. Saunders rose in the ranks of pro coaching, eventually being an NBA head coach for 17 years. Termini was his attorney and agent for the entire time.

"Flip was very confident, even when he was younger," said Termini. "I knew he'd become a big time coach. There was no doubt in his mind, or mine, that he'd do it."

Saunders went from Cuyahoga Heights—a small Ohio high school—to coaching in the NBA. He was never an NBA player. He worked his way up from a junior college head coach to a Division I college assistant. He became one of the most successful coaches in the history of the CBA (Continental Basketball Association, a minor league). Then, it was on to the NBA in 1995.

Ron Harper was one of Termini's early clients. *David I. Andersen / The Plain Dealer*

*   *   *

Termini loved his father and respected Marlo's dedication to his high school students and players. But he never saw himself in that role.

A year as an assistant to Flip at Golden Valley also convinced Termini college coaching was not his game.

He could have been a good coach. Termini is smart. He not only knew basketball as a coach's son, he had the heartbeat of the game inside him.

But Termini also has an independent streak.

"I wanted to control my own destiny," he said. "It's impossible to do that when you work for someone else."

He discovered that as he worked in sales for a downtown Cleveland hotel for a year right after college.

The next year he spent with Saunders in Minnesota. Then he returned to Cleveland to work for the Cavaliers during the Ted

Stepien days, selling tickets. In the 1980–81 media guide, he is listed as one of four "account executives."

How did he nab the job with the Cavaliers?

His father was also a very good softball player and coach. Stepien loved softball and had hired Marlo Termini as the general manager of his Cleveland Stepien's Competitors professional softball team.

Stepien had also followed Mark as a player at Holy Name and Case Western Reserve University and was familiar with his basketball accomplishments. When Stepien became the owner of the Cavs in 1980, that was an opening for Mark to interview for a job.

While he sold tickets, a big break that would shape his career was developing. He got to know Larry Creger, who was listed as the head of the Cavaliers player personnel department.

Actually, Creger was the team's head scout. Coach Bill Musselman and Stepien were making the key personnel decisions.

Creger also was in charge of the Los Angeles Summer Pro League. That was the forerunner to today's Las Vegas Summer League where NBA teams play games with rookies and marginal veterans looking to secure roster spots.

Termini helped Creger run the L.A. Summer League for two summers while he attended law school at Cleveland State University. That set him up to meet NBA general managers, coaches, scouts and some players.

He also met some agents.

In the early 1980s, there were far fewer agents than today. That started Termini seriously thinking about representing athletes as he approached graduation. By 1984, he had his law degree and attorney license.

*　　*　　*

Much like Saunders looked at coaching and thought, "I know I can do this," Termini had the same determination when it came to being successful as an agent.

One advantage to being exposed to executives, coaches and other agents at the L.A. Summer League was realizing he could play in the same business arena. Not all of the people he met were extraordinarily bright. Some were hired because of their basketball background, or merely because they were a part of the old guard. While he was with the Cavaliers, he sold Ted Stepien on establishing a series of summer basketball camps. Very few if any NBA teams had such camps at that time. Now most do.

While working for the Cavs, Termini also became friends with Scott Roth.

Roth was a best friend and teammate at Brecksville High School with Eric Musselman, the son of the Cavs head coach. Roth was hired by Termini to work for the Cavs camps as a counselor.

Following his law school graduation in 1984, Termini signed Roth as his first client. A star at Wisconsin, Roth eventually became a fourth-round pick of the San Antonio Spurs in the 1985 draft.

Roth ended up signing to play in Turkey that first year. He eventually worked his way to the NBA as a player and assistant coach.

Termini's next client was Brad Sellers, the Ohio State star from Warrensville Heights. He was another Cavs camp counselor hired by Termini. Then came Ron Harper, a Dayton native playing at Miami of Ohio.

With a pair of first round-picks in 1986, Termini was in the agent business. Along with Wendy Cohn, an attorney who became his partner and future wife, he established MTA Inc. (Mark Termini Associates).

They represented many of the best Ohio-based pro players such as Jimmy Jackson and Dennis Hopson (Ohio State), Earl Boykins (Cleveland Central Catholic), Dave Jamerson (Stow High, Ohio U.), Gary Trent (Ohio U.), John Edwards (Hudson High, Kent State), Jerome Lane (Akron St. Vincent-St. Mary) and Kosta Koufos (Canton GlenOak, Ohio State).

The revolutionary 1-and-1 contracts signed by LeBron James with the Cavaliers—two years guaranteed but with a one-year player option (or "out") the following season—were designed by Termini to maximize the earning power and leverage for the former Cavalier superstar.

Rich Paul was on the cover of Sports Illustrated in the summer of 2019. It was a well-deserved story about Paul, a relentless worker who is the face of the Klutch Sports Group. But the story barely mentioned Termini's role as the contract architect and negotiator.

A star client like James can attract players to his agency, but the agency has to deliver lucrative contracts. If not, other agents will swoop in and grab the players.

The bottom line is the bottom line, not simply the names of a few clients associated with an agent. Termini's advising and negotiating activities take place outside the media spotlight.

When James went to play for the Lakers, Paul moved his office to L.A. But Termini and his office remain in Brecksville.

"When Ron (Harper) was traded to the Clippers, I was watching a game while sitting courtside with (then-Clippers owner) Donald Sterling in L.A.," said Termini. "At halftime Donald stood up and looked at me with his arms spread wide. The Clippers girls were dancing behind him and he said, 'Mark, why do you want to stay in Cleveland? Everything is out here! Hollywood, pro sports. It all happens here!'"

Then Sterling said: "There's nothing in Cleveland for you, Mark, if you want to be big in this business!"

But that's not Termini. He's from here. He's stayed here.

"I'm from Cleveland," said Termini. "That's who I am."

CHAPTER 20

The Big "What If?"

What if the Cavaliers had never traded Ron Harper?

Would they have won a title?

Michael Jordan and the Chicago Bulls certainly don't think so. It was Jordan and the Bulls who knocked the Cavs out of the NBA playoffs five times, including twice with Harper (1988 and 1989) on the roster.

Some Cavs fans still debate it.

I tend to doubt even the talented Harper could have helped Cleveland overcome the Bulls.

Now I look back at the Harper/Danny Ferry deal as a sad chapter in Cavs history for both players involved. It was a quick decision that led to a hasty trade that haunted Ferry more than Harper, who had a terrific NBA career and played on five title teams with Chicago (3) and the L.A. Lakers (2).

For the Cavaliers, the deal was a disaster.

I'm writing this 30 years after the Nov. 16, 1989, trade.

As Harper's long-time friend and attorney Mark Termini told me: "Ron played 15 years in the NBA and earned five championship rings. That record speaks for itself."

Right after Harper was traded, he told me, "They (the Cavaliers) didn't like some of my friends."

That's really what the deal was about. The Cavs heard from the

NBA that some of Harper's friends allegedly were involved in the world of drugs. The Drug Enforcement Agency (DEA) was looking at some people who knew Harper.

Harper told the Cavs and the NBA he wasn't using drugs. The Cavs saw no indications of Harper using drugs. When the Cavs talked to Harper, he denied the drug rumors.

As Termini said, "Ron did have a different lifestyle and personality compared to some of the younger Cavs on the team at the time. But Ron was never late for meetings or flights. He never displayed even a hint of drug use before he was traded."

Nonetheless, the Cavs were afraid Harper was going to get into some type of trouble, based upon the rumors they heard. There was an internal meeting among owner Gordon Gund, general manager Wayne Embry and coach Lenny Wilkens.

When I helped Wilkens write his autobiography, he said ownership wanted him to "promise" there would be no trouble with Harper. As Wilkens explained, "Only God can do that."

Five months earlier, Cleveland Browns running back Kevin Mack was arrested on cocaine charges. Ten weeks before the Harper deal, Mack pleaded guilty to cocaine possession and served a month in jail.

It was an embarrassing situation for the Browns, and it was a hot topic in the media. The Cavaliers feared a public relations nightmare like that with Harper.

Embry didn't feel strong enough to oppose ownership when it came to trading Harper. He was very torn. He wanted to believe Harper, but also felt pressure from the NBA looking into Harper's associates.

More than once, Embry has told me, "I wish I had worked more with Mark (Termini) when all that hit."

Perhaps the Cavaliers would have had more clarity about Harper's associates and activities if they'd had a strong relationship with his agent and the player. It certainly would have been wiser to wait before making the decision to trade Harper.

But the Cavs didn't.

What followed was a rush to judgment that impacted the franchise for years.

*   *   *

When Embry began making calls to see who was interested in a gifted 6-foot-6 shooting guard averaging 22 points, 7.0 assists and 6.9 rebounds, many in the NBA were shocked. The season was only two weeks old.

That's an important fact: the season had just begun. Harper was only 25, entering his prime.

Embry tried to explain Harper was heading into free agency and it could be hard to sign him after the season. So the idea was to trade him now rather than have Harper walk away and the Cavs end up with nothing.

Few in the NBA believed that rationale.

Former NBA agent Ron Grinker often characterized statements like that as "accurate but not true."

It was accurate that Harper was heading to free agency and he was going to be expensive. After all, he was one of the best young players in the NBA.

But the truth was something else was driving the Cavs' desire to make the trade and most of the NBA knew it.

If they were going to trade him because of contract concerns, they would do it in the summer before his final season. Or maybe make a deal near the mid-season trading deadline. But the Cavs seemed in a frenzy to trade him only seven games into the season.

It made no sense to trade him so early into a very promising year for the young Cavaliers. Harper was a key member of the core group with Mark Price, Brad Daugherty, Hot Rod Williams and Larry Nance. They seemed poised to win the Eastern Conference, or at least contend with Detroit and Chicago.

The teams talking to the Cavs knew something must be very wrong with Harper. Or why the desperation to trade him so soon?

That's why the Cavs didn't have many attractive offers for Harper.

*   *   *

The Cavaliers found a taker for Harper in Los Angeles.

Not the Lakers, but the sad-sack Clippers. They had a real problem. After they made Duke star Danny Ferry the second pick in the 1989 draft, Ferry declined to sign with the franchise that had replaced Ted Stepien's Cavaliers as the most inept franchise in the NBA.

Ferry's father was Bob Ferry, who was the general manager of the Washington Bullets when his son entered the 1989 draft. The Ferry family hired David Falk, a high-powered agent whose clients included Michael Jordan, Patrick Ewing, Moses Malone and James Worthy.

The Ferry family wanted no part of the Clippers. They pushed for a trade. The Clippers thought Ferry could be a franchise-changing player, someone to stir fan interest in their team. The 6-foot-10 Ferry averaged 22.6 points, 7.4 rebounds and 4.7 assists as a senior with Duke. He shot .522 from the field, .425 from 3-point range.

The Clippers thought Ferry would eventually sign with them. What other option was there for him?

They thought wrong.

Falk cut a deal with a team in Rome, Il Messaggero Roma. They signed Ferry to a $2 million deal. He was given an expensive and exclusive 13th century piazza to live in. It had five stories. It was rent free.

The $2 million doesn't seem like much now. But in 1989, the highest paid player in Europe was former NBA star Bob McAdoo ($450,000). The Cavs' highest paid players were Brad Daugherty and Larry Nance at $1.1 million per year.

The franchise was owned by Raul Gardini, who was worth $25 billion in 1989. He didn't sell the 500 courtside seats. He gave them away to friends and business associates. He owned several companies and one of Rome's largest newspapers. The team didn't sell programs or souvenirs.

Ferry was given a BMW. The team supplied two maids to cook, clean and keep the huge piazza that he shared with the son of the team's owner.

Danny Ferry meets the press shortly after joining the Cavaliers. "I never was very athletic," said Ferry. "I was slow. I had to make up for it with skill." *Gus Chan / The Plain Dealer*

Falk made it clear to the Clippers that Ferry had no plans to sign with them, ever. He could keep playing in Italy and living in luxury.

Embry and the Cavaliers were enthralled with Ferry. They thought he'd at least be an All-Star. The idea of trading a popular and star player (Harper) would be easier for fans and the current Cavs players to accept if they could bring Ferry to Cleveland— even if Ferry made it clear he would not leave Rome until after the 1989–90 season.

The Cavs did not scout Ferry extensively in Italy. It's not like today's NBA where teams have several international scouts. I heard they talked to some people who saw him play in Rome, but that was it. No medical exams.

They couldn't even talk to him because Ferry was under contract in Rome, and as he told me, "There was no escape clause. I was finishing the season there."

The Cavs not only traded Harper to the Los Angeles Clippers, they also traded their first-round picks in 1990 and 1992. And they tossed in a second-round pick in 1991.

A member of the Cavs front office told me the draft picks were sort of "insurance" in case Harper had legal problems or the Clippers were not able to re-sign him after the 1989–90 season.

The Cavs made one of the worst statements in a press release quoting Wayne Embry:

"Trading Ron Harper was a tough decision. He is one of the top guards in the NBA. The chance to acquire the draft rights to Danny Ferry is an exceptional opportunity. The owners, coaches, staff and players have one goal—an NBA championship for Cleveland. Danny Ferry and Reggie Williams will help us get there.

"Boston waited a year for Larry Bird. San Antonio waited two years for David Robinson. You will see—Danny Ferry will be worth the wait."

No matter what the Cavaliers would later insist, they originally talked about Ferry as a future superstar. And they also armed his agent, David Falk, with power to negotiate a monster contract. This was before the NBA had a rookie contract scale, as is the case now.

The Cavs did receive 6-foot-7 guard Reggie Williams along with the rights to Ferry. But Williams became an NBA journeyman who played for six different teams in 10 seasons. He was a career 12-point scorer, but seemed lost when joining the Cavs after the Ferry deal. He played 32 games and then was waived by Cleveland.

*   *   *

Six weeks after the trade was announced, I visited Ferry in Rome for a series of stories for the Akron Beacon Journal.

Ferry was a gracious host. I had lunch at his villa. The "two maids" were actually middle-aged ladies who cooked and took care of the villa for Ferry and the son of the basketball team's owner. It was clear Ferry was homesick and that he'd sign with the Cavaliers.

Several times he told me he would not talk to the Cavs until his Italian season was over. He made that promise to his team in Rome.

The plan was for him to return to the NBA for the 1990–91 season.

I watched Ferry play and practice a few times, and his shooting and passing skills were obvious. Italian basketball was a slow-paced game. Most of the players had been pros for years. They did a lot of pushing, shoving and throwing elbows.

It didn't look much like the NBA game that featured fast breaks, athleticism and lively legs.

Ferry looked good, but he didn't dominate. For that season, he averaged 22 points and six rebounds. The Cavs promised Ferry they wouldn't bother him or even scout him in Italy. They didn't do so.

That was a mistake, because Ferry injured his knee while in Italy.

"We had an All-Star game and I banged knees with Bob McAdoo," Ferry told me in 2019. "I played through it. I knew something was wrong, but I wanted to finish the season."

Ferry didn't tell me that when I was in Italy. It does explain why I was surprised at his lack of mobility.

"I never was very athletic," said Ferry. "I was slow. I had to make up for it with skill."

I remember returning from Italy and watching some tapes of Ferry's games at Duke, where he was the NCAA Player of the Year for the 1988–89 season.

He didn't look like the same player.

*　　*　　*

After the Harper trade, the Cavs players were devastated. They'd heard the rumors about Harper, but saw nothing to support it. Harper was the same guy they knew from 1986, the guy who practiced hard, studied film and was on time for everything. They felt as if the trade sabotaged their season.

As Mark Price said, "We all came into the league together."

He meant Daugherty, Hot Rod Williams, Harper and himself. Craig Ehlo soon joined them as did Larry Nance. It was a close group. They took the trade personally. Their coach also was shell-shocked as Wilkens had to figure out who would play Harper's shooting guard spot. Making the situation worse, the Cavs had lost

Dell Curry (a natural replacement for Harper) in the 1989 summer expansion draft to Charlotte because they didn't protect him.

The Cavs opened that season on a four-game losing streak. But then they won three in a row . . . and Harper was traded.

They slogged through the year with a 42-40 record, a big drop from 57-25 in the previous season with Harper. They lost in the first round of the playoffs to Philadelphia.

*   *   *

After the season, the Cavaliers began negotiating with Falk to bring Ferry to Cleveland.

Because the Cavs and Ferry had an agreement not to have contact until after the season, I was the only one from Cleveland to spend time with him in Rome.

When I came home, several members of the Cavs organization asked me if Ferry would sign with them.

"No doubt," I said. "He grew up watching the NBA with his dad. He doesn't want to play in Italy. He has nothing against Cleveland. He'll sign."

But he did have the option to return to Rome, and his agent made that clear to the Cavaliers.

At this point, the Cavs had convinced themselves Ferry would be a great NBA player.

When the Cavs announced Ferry's signing, the details of a 10-year contract worth up to $40 million had not become public. At the press conference, Ferry said he understood the salary cap issues faced by teams and tried to help the Cavs in that area.

After the press conference, I asked owner Gordon Gund if Ferry "left some money on the table" during the contract talks.

"Maybe," said Gund. "But not much."

The deal also included a clause whereby the Cavaliers would "own" Ferry's marketing rights, meaning they'd receive cash if he became a big star such as Bird.

Falk hammered the Cavaliers in these contract talks with Ferry suddenly making more than twice as much as anyone on Cleveland roster. His first year salary was $2.6 million.

That wasn't all.

A few months later, Hot Rod Williams received a seven-year, $26 million offer sheet from Miami. It was front-loaded with Williams receiving $9 million in the first 12 months.

Why did Miami give Williams a deal making him the NBA's highest paid player?

Because the Heat believed the Cavs would not match it after paying big for Ferry. And the Williams camp believed the Cavs were not making him a reasonable offer because of what they paid Ferry.

The Ferry contract kept costing the Cavs more money.

They matched the offer sheet to keep Williams. He became the team's highest paid player. Ferry was No. 2.

And Price, Daugherty and Nance were All-Stars.

This led to the Cavs quietly reworking the deals for those three core players. The Cavs had the NBA's highest payroll for the 1990–91 season at $14.3 million. The NBA salary cap figure was $11.8 million.

*   *   *

This might have worked out if Ferry indeed became a star.

But he was going to the wrong team. The Cavaliers didn't need another 6-foot-10 player. They had Daugherty (7-foot), Williams (6-foot-11) and Nance (6-foot-10). The Cavs thought Ferry could play small forward, but that didn't work. He wasn't quick enough defensively.

In the modern NBA, Ferry would be a "stretch-4," a power forward who can "stretch" the defense by making 3-point shots. But the NBA of the 1990s wasn't about big men shooting from long distances.

Meanwhile, Ferry's knee wasn't 100% from the injury in Italy. He kept playing through it, wanting to help the Cavaliers.

"The contract didn't weigh on me that much," said Ferry. "It was more my expectations and other people's expectations. I felt like I was letting myself down. I felt like I was letting others down. That led to me putting more and more pressure on myself."

Pressure was bubbling up in the Cavalier locker room.

For a year, the Cavs veterans had been hearing about Ferry and how he was supposed to be a franchise-changing player. They saw the Cavaliers pay him that way. But on the court, he struggled to create his own shot. He was vulnerable on defense, especially attempting to guard smaller, more athletic players at small forward.

Wilkens was receiving subtle pressure to play Ferry, but the coach had a hard time finding minutes. Ferry wasn't better than Williams, Nance or Daugherty. He was ill-equipped to play small forward. Wilkens started second-year players Chucky Brown and Winston Bennett at small forward.

Ferry played 20 minutes a game, averaging 8.6 points and 3.5 rebounds. He shot a mediocre .428 from the field, .299 on 3-point shots. He led the team in personal fouls per minutes because of his struggles on defense.

After that season, he had knee surgery.

"It was a microfracture," he said. "I had a nickel-sized hole in the cartilage."

That's major surgery and few players come all the way back from it. In his second season, Ferry seemed even worse than as a rookie. He was slower. His confidence remained shaken.

The 20.5 minutes per game Ferry played as a rookie was the most he'd be on the court in the first five years of his career.

One season, the Cavs asked him to bulk up and play center.

"I went from 225 pounds to 265," said Ferry. "That wasn't healthy for me."

When Ferry played, he refused to mention any knee problems. His surgeries were in the off-season and kept quiet. He didn't want anyone to think he was making excuses for his poor play.

"It started in Italy when I banged knees," he said. "That caused a bone bruise. I kept playing on it and that caused trauma to the knee. The contusion in the knee became a hole. That led to the first surgery."

Ferry isn't sure how many surgeries he had in his career.

"I think it's five," he said. "I had them in both knees."

In 1995–96, the Cavaliers roster was entirely different from the

"Trading Ron Harper was a tough decision," Cavs GM Wayne Embry said at the time. If the Cavs hadn't made that trade, would they have won a title?
Richard T. Conway / The Plain Dealer

team Ferry joined in 1989. He was given a chance to start, averaging 13.3 points and shooting .459 from the field. It would be the best season of his 13-year career.

Ferry made himself into a role player, a big man coming off the bench to hustle for rebounds and shoot from the outside. His last three seasons (2000–03) were with the San Antonio Spurs, where he was part of a championship team in 2003.

*   *   *

It's like everyone in this trade was cursed.

About the same time Ferry injured his knee in Italy, Harper had a major knee injury with the Clippers. On Jan. 18, 1990, Harper caught a pass from teammate Gary Grant. As he planted his right knee, it collapsed. He fell to the court.

Harper had suffered a major anterior cruciate ligament (ACL) injury. This required reconstructive knee surgery. Harper had played only 28 games for the Clippers, averaging 23 points, 5.6 rebounds and 4.8 assists.

Harper was hoping for a big payday as a free agent, but the injury and surgery destroyed that possibility. Harper eventually signed a four-year, $9.75 million deal with the Clippers. He missed a calendar year before he returned to the court.

It took nine months to work out the deal. While Harper was still in the hospital recovering from knee surgery, Clippers owner Donald Sterling called to make an offer for the next season.

"It's $200,000," said Sterling. "That's what the President of the United States makes!"

But Harper was already being paid $650,000 for the season in which he was traded and suffered the knee injury.

Termini and Harper turned down the chance to make a few more bucks than the president.

Termini did a masterful job negotiating that contract for the injured Harper. In the final season (1993–94), Harper was to be paid the same $4 million as Michael Jordan was to make under his contract.

In five years with the Clippers, he was a 19.3 point scorer. He was still a very good player, but the knee injury robbed Harper of some of his athleticism.

The remarkable part of Harper's career is how he re-invented himself after the knee surgery. He became a better passer, defender and improved his outside shot. He left the Clippers as a free agent and signed with Chicago ($19.2 million over five years), where he played on three title-winning teams with Michael Jordan.

Bulls coach Phil Jackson fell in love with Harper for his leadership and knowledge of the game. When Jackson left the Bulls for the Lakers, he took Harper with him.

His career spanned 15 seasons. He never was in any trouble. The trade to the Clippers worked out well for him in the long run because it eventually led to Chicago and the Lakers—where Harper became a championship caliber player.

Harper made about $40 million in his NBA career thanks to some excellent contracts and his Nike shoe deal. In the end, he had a good basketball life.

*   *   *

As for Ferry, it seems as if he would have been better off signing with the Clippers. Maybe he still would have injured his knee. But it would have happened in the USA, not Italy. Perhaps he would have sought treatment earlier.

Nor would he have been in the same pressure cooker with the Clippers as he was in Cleveland. He also would have joined a bad team (21-61 record) that would have created playing time for him.

Ferry still doesn't second-guess himself about Italy.

"It was the right thing for my career at the time," said Ferry. "But when I got over there, it seemed to take away any momentum I had after college. Then I got hurt."

Ferry remains grateful to former teammates such as Nance, Williams, Daugherty, Price and the rest. He knows on some teams, he would have been shunned or ridiculed because his production didn't come close to matching his contract.

It wouldn't have mattered that Ferry had no personal part in the decision to trade Harper. Nor is it Ferry's fault the Cavaliers decided to pay him like the next Larry Bird.

"Those guys were great to me," he said. "They knew how hard I worked and how much I cared. Wayne Embry brought in guys with high character. They were team-first guys and they were about winning. They were great teammates, they treated me wonderfully."

That's part of the reason Ferry has warm feelings about Cleveland.

"It's a great sports city with terrific people," he said. "I felt accepted there."

Ferry admits, "I beat myself up. I so wanted to be a good player. It was the first time in my life basketball didn't come easy. My dream was to play in the NBA. I had to really work to find my place in the league."

Ferry returned to Cleveland in 2005 to become the team's general manager. He had that job for five years.

"Cleveland is a great place," he said. "I value the friends I made there. The fans came to accept me. I didn't live up to my own expectations or anyone else's. For a while, I dwelled on that. But eventually, I got healthier. I found a way to help the team. I enjoyed that. Overall, I cherish my time in Cleveland, I really do."

Fans Write In . . .

Favorite Memories

When I was in third grade, my regular school bus driver was out sick and we had a substitute who noticed my Cavaliers coat and hat. I would sit at the front of the bus and talk about the Cavs with her every morning. I was sad when the driver told me our regular driver would be coming back. She had a present for me on the last day—an autographed 8x10 of Cavs guard Gerald Wilkins. It read, "Joel, thanks for behaving on the bus. Keep up the good work!" It was one of the few times I cried in life because I was happy.

—*Joel Voorman, Canton, Ohio*

I was a huge fan during the Lenny Wilkens years. I didn't know much about pro basketball, but I happened to catch a game one night in 1989 on TV. It was mesmerizing. Seeing the play and teamwork between Brad Daugherty and Mark Price was like watching a ballet—athletic, perfectly timed, graceful and beautiful. I watched every game that I could; I voraciously read every article (many by you) in the Beacon Journal. I listened to Joe Tait on the radio. My favorite player was Mark, but I loved Brad, Hot Rod Williams, Craig Ehlo and Gerald Wilkins, too.

When I think of those halcyon years during Lenny's tenure, I don't think of The Shot or injuries or playoffs and rings not won. I think of a team that played beautiful ball unselfishly. My prevailing thought is of "Mark Price for THREEEEEEEE!" ringing from the rafters.

—*Cheryle Robinson, Columbus, Ohio*

While in college in the early '80s, I was commuting my last two years from the middle of the snow belt (Geneva) to Kent State's main campus. They were very long days in the computer lab and driving home exhausted, late at night in a junky old Ford Pinto wagon. It was 1½ to 2½ hours each direction, depending on the snow.

During many dark and cold nights I would look forward to hearing Joe Tait. There was Roy Hinson crashing the boards, John Bagley dribbling, Phil Hubbard and Lonnie Shelton putting on their hard hats and going to work . . . and of course, World B. Free for THREE!

Listening to games made that long drive much more enjoyable. The nights they didn't play, the drive was tougher and I would struggle to stay awake. I would even work later in the computer lab when they had West Coast games just so I could listen on the way home. Joe and the Cavs helped get me through college.

—*Mario Perkins, Macedonia, Ohio*

Near the end of one of those wild playoff games during the Miracle of Richfield, there was a timeout and it was impossible to hear anything. After talking to his players, Cavs coach Bill Fitch pointed at Nate Thurmond. As Nate stood up, he started peeling off his warm-up and the volume from the crowd seemed to triple, like the sound behind a jet engine.

—*Robert C. Petti, Twinsburg, Ohio*

Listening to Joe Tait on 3WE was the only way to enjoy the Cavs from 100 miles away in Erie, Pa. Bobby "Bingo" Smith became a favorite as Joe painted the picture of a Bingo catch-and-shoot bomb from the corner, over and over in the Cavaliers' wine and gold, going east to west on your radio dial.

—*Tom Yochim, Erie, Pennsylvania*

I was a girl who lived in a predominantly male neighborhood and was "allowed" to play some sports activities with the boys. I was a good runner and could bat fairly well. Being a southpaw, I found catching with a right-hand mitt challenging. When I reached my teens, the boys preferred that I watch from the sidelines or be their cheerleader. No fun!

In 1965, I saw the Harlem Globetrotters play, and they were unbelievable. I had never been to a professional game, but I was hooked on basketball. Growing up when I did—graduating from high school in '65—girls didn't play basketball in physical education classes. It was just field hockey or "cut-throat, smash-in-your-face" volleyball. That quickly cured me of any interest in that sport. Ugh!

Then my family moved to Cleveland, and I got to see the Cavs play my favorite sport at the Coliseum while I was finishing my studies at Cleveland State University during the 1970s. I have been to the arena downtown, but there was some emotional tie about going to see the Cavs in Richfield.

—*Sharen Morris-Allen, Elyria, Ohio*

I remember being at my grandmother's house for the Miracle of Richfield. I was 9 years old and knew who the Cavs were, but I had never seen my Polish immigrant grandmother so excited! She was yelling in Polish and broken English. She has been gone for many years, but when I hear of the Miracle of Richfield, my 9-year-old self remembers my Gram!

—*Adam Witczak, Garfield Heights, Ohio*

I remember some of Joe Tait's signature phrases, such as, "A whistle and . . . what?" like he was slightly annoyed that an official had stopped play for no worthwhile reason. Because of Joe, I referred to the half-court line as the "time line." Hearing Joe sign off with, "Have a GOOD niiiiight, everybody!" was my cue to finally go to bed. I teared up when in his final broadcast, he signed off with, "Have a GOOD liiiife, everybody!"

—*Tom Pestak, Xenia, Ohio*

My husband, Bill, was a Cavaliers fan forever. He was a teacher and football and basketball coach at Niles McKinley High School, and, being very thrifty, when he could afford Cavs tickets became a season ticket holder with the cheapest available, $10 per game.

Bill and his friend Jim loved going to games. They would take turns driving from Niles to the Coliseum. When the Cavs moved to downtown, they would drive to the Green station of the RTA (free parking) and take the train to the arena ($1.50 each way, I think). When the Cavs moved, season ticket holders had the opportunity to visit the Gund and choose their seats. Bill went to Section 233 (directly behind the basket and way, way up) and chose Row 1, Seat 1. The ticket was $10 (including tax!). Bill and I always laughed because his $10 seat was right above some of the very expensive loges, but that had almost exactly the same view of the game.

Those $10 ticket holders were treated royally by the Cavs. Bill had those $10 season tickets until his death in 1999, and the Cavs love continues in our family.

—*Patricia Pfeifer, Niles, Ohio*

The best Coliseum memory was when the Cavs beat the Jazz as Craig Ehlo hit the game-winning shot. My dad, my brother and I were at the game. We could not wait to get to the car and hear Joe Tait's call of the shot replayed on the post-game show. He yelled out, "Yes, Virginia, there is a Santa Claus and he comes from Lubbock, Texas (Ehlo's home-town)."

—*John Houser, Portales, New Mexico*

When I was 10 years old in 1991, I remember being so pumped hearing Joe Tait: "Three on the way. Got it! Or, "Wham with the right hand!" I went to Game 7 in 1992 against the Boston Celtics with my dad, the first game we ever went to together. He was not born in the U.S., but loved those Cavs teams—even more than the LeBron teams.

—*Cory Jarrous, Lakewood, Ohio*

I remember World B. Free shot a 3-pointer and made it and the referee did not notice where his feet were. He signaled a 2-point shot. Free got very upset, stole the ball immediately and came back to the exact same spot. He pointed down to his feet and put up the ball and made the three again. It was hilarious.

—*Jeff Shibley, Kirtland Hills, Ohio*

I attended three playoff games during the Miracle of Richfield season. I recently watched highlights of those games on YouTube and it still gave me goosebumps! The amazing thing is how easy it was to buy game tickets.

—*Don Moore, Cortland, Ohio*

We had a radio intercom system in our house, and the central control unit was in the kitchen, always tuned to 3WE. Pete Franklin ruled the airwaves unless there was a game being broadcast. Much of the time, my mom and I were right there with him. As a kid, I didn't try to separate the showmanship from the legitimate sports reporting. It was all legitimate reporting to me!

His stable of regular callers included The Swami, the Canoga Park Creep and Mr. Know-It-All, who we all now know as Mike Trivisonno. They made many an appearance after a game. Pete jousted with them all. It was often a different Pete Franklin who interviewed coaches such as Bill Fitch. He was almost pandering, and clearly supportive. I remember Pete supporting the then-controversial draft pick of Jim Brewer. Pete had Bill on the show to explain it to the fans.

Pete often boasted about the strong signal of the radio station, saying he could be heard in 38 states and half of Canada. Every now and then, it would take a caller from the middle of nowhere in Canada just to prove his point. We took a family vacation way up in northern Ontario one summer and proved him right. What I remember most of Pete's shows was the ending. He would usher in Jimmy Durante singing, "Good night," by saying, "I see that my time is up, thank you very much for your time." A drop of humility, but it worked!

—*Vince Granieri, Cincinnati, Ohio*

During Game 7 of the 1976 Cavs-Bullets playoff series, I was working in the sports department of the Salem News in Salem, Ohio. I was done working at 9 p.m. with the game well into the second half. I drove from Salem to Austintown to meet my friend Paul, who was at home mending a broken ankle.

On the way, Dick Snyder hit the game-winning shot. There was no one who could make a game-winner sound better than Joe Tait. I was quite excited that the Cavs had advanced in the playoffs. I arrived at Paul's apartment and rang the doorbell. He came to the door and picked me up and swung me around like a rag doll. Paul was about 6-foot-3 and 225 pounds to my 5-foot-11 and 175 pounds. This was a man standing in a walking cast doing the delirious swinging. I will never forget that night, that scene and my best friend. I am sorry he passed in 2010 and never got to see our beloved Cavaliers win the NBA title in 2016.

   —*Ed Warren, Lyndhurst, Ohio*

   I was a ball boy for the New Orleans Jazz from 1975 to 1979. Once, I was asked to come in early and help the Cavs with their team shoot-around. Usually, the ball boy who sat on the visitor's bench would go to the shoot around, but he was unavailable. I wore a shirt with my nickname, Moose, on the back. All the players would call for me by saying, "Mooooose!"

   After that, whenever the Cavs came to town I would help at the shoot-around. I sat on their bench and worked in their locker room each time they visited us.

   The Cavs players, coaches and staff, including Joe Tait, Charlie Strasser and Bill Fitch treated me like one of their own and I have never forgotten that. The Cavaliers were the only team I would leave the Jazz bench for and sit on their bench for games.

   Once the trainer (Charlie Strasser) had me wash their uniforms after a game at my house because the Cavs had back-to-back games and were staying overnight in New Orleans. Charlie kept saying, "Make sure you don't bleach the uniforms!" I was a high school kid at the time. Imagine the trust they had in me. My mom and I did the laundry until the early hours of the morning, then I dropped them off at the team hotel.

   I have signed pennants from the Cavaliers in those years. Great memories. Go Cavs!

   —*David Musso, Balboa, California*

CHAPTER 21

Wayne Embry, Lenny Wilkens and Greatness

I was sitting with Wayne Embry, who was a consultant with the Toronto Raptors. The LeBron James Era Cavaliers were facing Toronto for the third time in the playoffs. It was about three hours before the game.

"Wayne, you know you have no chance," I said.

It wasn't meant to be arrogant.

"Greatness," I said.

Embry smiled and sadly shook his head.

"Number 23 is very good," said Embry.

"Greatness," I repeated.

"Greatness," he said.

Number 23 was LeBron James during those 2018 playoffs.

But Embry and I were thinking about another Number 23 and another time.

From 1988 to 1994, the Cavaliers were eliminated five times by Michael Jordan and the Chicago Bulls. Embry was the Cavs general manager for all of that. Lenny Wilkens was the coach for each series except the final one in 1994.

After a while, Embry would simply say, "Greatness" when the subject of Jordan came up.

When they faced James in the playoffs, the Raptors had built a team much like Embry's Cavaliers—good but not great. They faced the Cavs three times in the playoffs, and were wiped out each time by James.

That changed in the 2019 playoffs when James left Cleveland for the L.A. Lakers. The Raptors made a bold trade for Kawhi Leonard. With James out of the Eastern Conference, Leonard led the Raptors to the title.

Embry and I talked about greatness.

Basketball is a team sport but played by only five at a time. One player can dominate a game. You can assemble a gifted, unselfish team that plays beautiful basketball. But a pretty good team with a player for the ages—"greatness"—will usually prevail in a best-of-7 series.

From 2014–18, the Cavaliers had James—the best player in the world.

From 2010–14, Miami had James—the best player in the world.

No one else in the Eastern Conference had a player who could come close to matching James.

In those eight years, James led his teams to eight consecutive NBA Finals as he frustrated Toronto and everyone else in the Eastern Conference trying to beat him. It was only in the NBA Finals when he faced teams such as Golden State or San Antonio with their own future Hall of Famers that James was defeated.

"I felt it when I was a player with the (Cincinnati) Royals," said Embry. "We had Oscar Robertson. A great player. But we couldn't get past Russ (Bill Russell) and the Celtics."

Three times his Royals were knocked out of the playoffs by Boston. Robertson was one the best guards ever. Embry made five All-Star teams as a center. But Russell won 11 NBA titles in his 13-year career.

Greatness.

Suppose the Cavaliers had not made the Ron Harper/Danny Ferry deal. Would they have won a title with Harper?

"I don't know," said Embry. "Once Michael got going, who did beat him?"

Jordan went to the NBA Finals six times and won six titles.

Greatness.

Cavs head coach Lenny Wilkens and general manager Wayne Embry discuss their selection in the 1988 NBA Draft. They put together excellent teams—but ran into Michael Jordan. *Ralph J. Meyers / The Plain Dealer*

The Cavaliers of the Wayne Embry/Lenny Wilkens Era didn't have it.

But oh my, they had some very, very good teams.

*   *   *

I began covering the Cavaliers at the start of the 1985–86 season.

I caught a break when Larry Pantages wanted to leave the NBA beat and join the business news department of the Akron Beacon Journal. Executives Dale Allen and Tom Giffen offered me the job.

I jumped at it.

After covering baseball for six years, I was looking for something different. I've always loved basketball. The Cavaliers were coming off a trip to the 1985 playoffs. They had a young coach in George Karl. They had a sharp general manager in Harry Weltman. They had a star in World B. Free, who was fun to watch and interview. I thought they'd have a good season.

As often happens with me, I thought wrong.

Early in the season, Karl was fighting with Weltman over a contract extension. Karl was only 34 years old. He conveniently forgot how Weltman gave him his first chance to be a head coach in the NBA, and then supported him when the 1984–85 season started 2-19.

Karl admired Don Nelson, who was then the coach of the Milwaukee Bucks and also had the powers of the general manager. Karl saw himself in that role. Looking back, he was too immature, his ego too big for him to be patient. He clashed with Weltman.

Meanwhile, Weltman was unhappy with Karl for not wanting to use some of his young players.

Karl and Free never were thrilled with each other in the best of times. Soon those hostilities bubbled to the surface.

It didn't take long for Karl to privately blame the players and the front office for his problems. Weltman and some of the players heard about it.

The team was losing. Weltman thought Karl could do a better job coaching. Karl thought Weltman didn't give him enough talent to win.

Some players felt Karl was "scapeboating" them.

That's right . . . "scapeboating."

As Cavalier center Mel Turpin told me, "I ain't gonna be no scapeboat around here."

He meant "scapegoat," but came close enough for me to understand the real split between Karl and some players.

It was a mess.

And it was a mess only a few years removed from the Ted Stepien disaster.

Karl was fired by Weltman with 15 games left in the season. He was replaced by Gene Littles, who *three* times in his NBA career served as an interim head coach.

Littles, a wonderful man, once told me, "They should put '*interim*' on my tombstone."

Owner Gordon Gund was disenchanted by the Karl/Weltman conflict. By nature, he is a man who prefers stability. The day after the season ended, when Weltman had returned from a scouting trip, the general manager was fired.

In another chapter, I explained how the Cavaliers pulled off an amazing 1986 draft without a general manager or coach in place. But as I wrote right after that draft, "Embry had his fingerprints all over it."

*   *   *

Embry took over the Cavs after the 1986 draft. He went looking for a coach.

A few months earlier, Lenny Wilkens had approached Embry at the Big East college basketball tournament in the spring of 1986. Wilkens had been removed as the coach of the Seattle SuperSonics after the 1984–85 season, but the team named him general manager.

Wilkens knew he didn't have a long future in the front office with that Seattle ownership group. He also believed he was more wired for coaching.

Meanwhile, Embry was a consultant for the Indiana Pacers. He had been the general manager for the Milwaukee Bucks in 1972— the first black general manager in NBA history. But he eventually lost a power struggle to Bucks coach Don Nelson.

So when Wilkens and Embry talked at that Big East Tournament, both of their careers had sagged.

Wilkens was a Hall of Fame point guard. He coached Seattle to the 1979 NBA title. But he had a 31-51 record in his last season as Seattle's head coach.

Embry was looking for a chance to be a general manager again.

"People often assumed Lenny and I were friends," said Embry. "We played against each other. We knew each other to say hello and talk a bit. But you'd never consider us friends."

So Wilkens was not trying to convince a buddy to hire him, assuming Embry did become a general manager again.

"Wayne, if you get back (as a GM), think of me," said Wilkens. "I miss coaching."

Embry said he'd keep it in mind, but he didn't know if he'd have another chance to be a general manager.

Then Gund and the Cavaliers came along.

Embry had a point in the interviewing process when he nearly backed out. One of the people interviewing him for the Cavs—not Gund—asked Embry if he felt compelled to hire a black coach.

Embry was understandably insulted.

"Would they ask a white general manager if he was going to hire a white coach?" Embry wondered.

Embry told me that story several times. He deals with it in depth in his 2004 book "The Inside Game: Race, Power and Politics in the NBA," written with Mary Schmitt Boyer.

Gund later assured Embry that was not his view. He just wanted the best coach Embry could hire.

Embry said that was his goal.

Bill Fitch coached the Cavaliers from 1970 to 1979.

One coach for nine seasons.

Then the Cavaliers went through *eight* coaches in the next *seven* years.

That's right, *eight* coaches in *seven* years.

*　　*　　*

Embry interviewed NBA assistant coaches Dick Harter, Ed Badger and John Wetzel along with Wilkens.

The finalists were Wilkens and Wetzel. Why Wetzel? He interviewed well and was given a strong endorsement by Jerry Colangelo, the general manager of the Phoenix Suns and a close friend of Embry. But Wetzel had never been a head coach at any level. In my stories, I pushed hard for the hiring of Wilkens. Embry decided Wilkens was both the wisest and safest choice. This was not a situation for a rookie head coach.

The Cavaliers needed maturity and experience in those two key spots. Embry and Wilkens represented those qualities. Wilkens had played for the Cavaliers (1972–74). Fans knew him and respected him.

Embry and Wilkens shared the same values and moral center. They wanted to build a team with good people. They wanted to play team, unselfish basketball. They also savored a second chance to prove to the teams that had cast them aside that they could build a winner in Cleveland.

"There had been too much turmoil," said Embry. "To build a team with young players, you can't have that. Lenny and I agreed on that point. As I got to know Lenny (during the coaching interviews), I knew we could work together."

Quietly, the Embry/Wilkens combination became the first NBA team with African-Americans in those crucial positions. It also was done for the right reasons. Not to make a racial statement, but because they were the best candidates available.

And they proved it during their years together.

*   *   *

I talked to Embry several times while writing this book.

He kept saying to mention that Harry Weltman did a good job bringing the Cavs out of the Stepien ownership era. Weltman drafted Roy Hinson, who was used in the trade for Brad Daugherty in 1986.

Weltman's biggest gamble was drafting John "Hot Rod" Williams in 1985. Embry never would have taken that chance. The NBA even sent out a memo before the draft suggesting teams stay away from Williams, who had been implicated in the Tulane point-shaving scandal.

Williams was exonerated in time for the beginning of the Embry/Wilkens Era.

"Harry gave us a terrific player," said Embry. "Hot Rod was a great guy. He fit in well with the others we had."

When Wilkens opened training camp in the fall of 1986, he had four promising rookies: Ron Harper, Mark Price, Daugherty and Williams. The Cavs also had a fifth in Johnny Newman. He played only one season with the Cavaliers, but 16 total in the NBA.

Embry later signed Craig Ehlo from the Mississippi Jets of what was then called the Continental Basketball Association (CBA). Guess who owned that team? Ted Stepien! You can't make this stuff up.

He made a huge trade on Feb. 25, 1988. The key players were rookie point guard Kevin Johnson going to Phoenix for veteran forward Larry Nance.

"We not only wanted to add talent, but also character," said Embry. "KJ (Kevin Johnson) was going to be a great player. But he was stuck behind Mark Price. We had so many young guys, we needed a veteran to be a leader. That was Larry."

At first, Nance was upset about leaving Phoenix. But once he joined the Cavs, he realized his Southern roots (Anderson, South Carolina) put him in a comfort zone with most of the Cavs players.

Embry and Wilkens were carefully picking athletes and people to shape the type of team they wanted on and off the court.

*   *   *

I covered the Cavaliers on a daily basis for all seven years of Wilkens as coach.

Most practices were open to the media. Watching them was like going to basketball graduate school.

Wilkens has a degree in economics from Providence. He likes numbers and math. He viewed some passes like geometry problems. The same with floor spacing.

His plays were designed to create room for players to drive to the basket. He didn't want three or four players hanging around the same part of the court as if waiting for a bus on the corner. The ball moves faster than a player can run, so pass it.

One day, I asked Wilkens why he designed in-bounds plays for the man passing the ball to get it back for a shot.

This was after practice.

Wilkens grabbed a basketball. He walked to the sidelines.

"I'm going to in-bound the ball," he said. "You guard me."

Wilkens stood on the sidelines. He had me raise my arms, waving to make it hard for him to throw an in-bounds pass.

He fired the ball past my ear. My head turned to see where the ball went. Then I turned back to where Wilkens had been standing, but he was gone.

He had moved to the middle of the court.

"See what happens," he said. "When the man passes the ball, the defender watches it and loses sight of the man he is supposed to be guarding. Then that man is open for a return pass."

Many fans remember Jordan making The Shot to eliminate the Cavs in the 1989 playoffs. The Bulls had the ball with three seconds left because the Cavaliers had just scored.

How did they score?

With six seconds left, Wilkens called time out. He set up a play with Craig Ehlo throwing the in-bounds pass. He had Nance at the opposite side of the court. Nance ran in the direction of Ehlo, who threw him the ball.

Then Ehlo cut hard to the rim . . . and Nance threw it back to Ehlo for a layup.

The Chicago defender did the same thing guarding Ehlo as I did when I guarded Wilkens. He turned his head and lost sight of the man he was supposed to be defending. Three seconds later, Ehlo scored.

"We scored too fast," said Ehlo. "Too bad I didn't hang in the air for three more seconds."

The same idea was behind a game-winning shot against Utah on Dec. 23, 1991.

This time, Nance ran along the baseline and caught a pass in the corner. Ehlo took a pair of quick steps, stopping at the 3-point line. Nance threw the ball back to him . . . swish!

Three points, Cavs win.

That was the game when Joe Tait told his radio audience: "Yes, Virginia, there is a Santa Claus and he comes from Lubbock, Texas!"

Ehlo grew up in Lubbock.

"I still don't know where that (call) came from," Tait said years later.

Price told me how he learned so much of the game from Wilkens.

They both were cerebral point guards. They both were considered "too small" when they came into the NBA. They both brought out the best in each other.

While playing for Wilkens was difficult for Ferry simply because he was dealing with bad knees and little playing time was available to him, Ferry said the coach "was great with in-game adjustments and out-of-bounds plays."

The Cavs had a very smart, thoughtful coach and their team reflected his style.

*   *   *

Wilkens had records of 57-25 and 54-28 in his final two seasons as coach. They were the best regular season back-to-back records in team history to that point.

But in both seasons, the Cavs were eliminated by the Bulls in the playoffs. As the front office and ownership were discussing if they should bring Wilkens back for another season, Wilkens decided to resign.

He believed he had done everything possible with the Cavaliers. The success had been over-ridden by the frustration of losing to Jordan.

He thought the Cavs could use "a new voice" and he could use a new challenge. That led to the Cavs hiring Mike Fratello while Atlanta jumped at the chance to name Wilkens its head coach.

Wilkens coached the Hawks for the next seven seasons, having six winning records. He was an NBA coach for 32 years for six different teams when he retired at the age of 67.

Embry and Wilkens were together for seven years, the longest GM/coach combination in franchise history.

Embry and Wilkens came along when the franchise desperately needed a sense of purpose and a strong dose of character. They brought in good players and very good people. For those of us who watched those teams, that meant a lot.

CHAPTER 22

My Favorite Era

I loved the Cavaliers of the late 1980s and early 1990s.

Let's call it the Mark Price, Brad Daugherty, Larry Nance and John "Hot Rod" Williams Era.

Can you still love a team that doesn't win a title? A team that never even reached the NBA Finals?

Why not?

Sports should not simply be "winner take all," at least when it comes to the hearts of the fans and the players.

"We connected with our fans," said Mark Price. "I know we didn't win a title. But we had some terrific teams, You could feel it at the old (Richfield) Coliseum. The fans related to us."

Why?

"I think it was because we were regular guys," said Price.

This was the late 1980s and early 1990s. Players didn't have entourages. They made big money for the time, but nothing like today.

"We used to go to a playground called Valley Vista (in Cuyahoga Falls)," said Price. "Craig (Ehlo), Bags (John Bagley) and some other guys from the team would play pick-up ball in the summer with some guys who just came to the park to play."

It was a different time.

The media was permitted to watch practice, which was held in a small gym on the top level of the Coliseum. When practice was over, some members of the media would play pick-up games.

At times, players sitting on the bench for the Cavs would join us. They wanted to run full court. On a few occasions, I played in the same backcourt as Steve Kerr. I had one job—throw the ball to Kerr. He was practicing moving without the ball, curling around picks, coming free for a pass.

Then I was supposed to dribble the ball up the court and deliver a pass so he could catch it and quickly fire up a 3-pointer.

It was done in the context of a full court game.

Who knew Kerr would become one of the greatest coaches in NBA history? At that point, he was a backup guard just hoping to stay in the NBA.

One day, Kerr and I went to lunch. He was worried about being cut. I told him to relax, they were going to keep him on the roster.

"How do you know?" he asked.

I said that Lenny Wilkens and Wayne Embry love shooters. They had just traded a second-round pick to Phoenix for him. They valued his long-range shooting. They weren't going to cut him so soon.

"I hope you're right," he said.

"I'm right," I said. "In fact, you are going to play 10 years in the NBA. And when you do, you buy me lunch."

Kerr played 15 seasons in the NBA. He was on five NBA title teams. When he was with the Bulls and helped win three titles during the Jordan Era, he indeed bought me lunch.

But back then, he was a scared player in his second NBA season wondering if he belonged. He had spent the summer dribbling around chairs to improve his ball handling. He was in post-practice pick-up games with a few teammates, Cavs front office people and sportswriters just so he could improve some of the weak parts of his game.

We'd play with Chris Dudley, Winston Bennett, Chucky Brown, Kerr and others. Usually, there were four pros in the game—two on each team. They'd defend each other. For the most part, we ran up and down the court and tried to stay out of their way.

As Price said, "We saw ourselves as regular guys."

Brad Daugherty shouts encouragement to Larry Nance after scoring during a game in 1990. *Curt Chandler / The Plain Dealer*

*   *   *

The Richfield Coliseum was the perfect place for this team to play. Some media people called it "The Big House on the Prairie" because it was next to the Cuyahoga Valley National Park on one side. A small sheep farm was on the other.

"Most of us were from small towns," said Price. "We liked the Coliseum being in Richfield."

I remember Hot Rod Williams telling me how living in Copley and playing at the Coliseum reminded him of growing up in Sorrento, Louisiana. Williams died of cancer in 2015.

I interviewed him and several other Cavaliers for a story about where they learned to play basketball. That was in 1988 when I was with the Akron Beacon Journal.

Williams said: "My basket was an old bicycle rim. We knocked out the spokes and nailed it to a tree. The court was really dirt with rocks. After I was done playing, my socks were black from the dirt and filled with sand."

Mike Sanders grew up in Vidalia, Louisiana. His mother picked cotton when Sanders was young. She'd take him to the fields with her. Later, she got a job at a hospital. It was next to a playground with lights and a concrete surface.

Daugherty grew up in Black Mountain, North Carolina. He said his first rim was about 9 feet off the ground, nailed to an oak tree. There were some tall bushes near the court. Daugherty shot over them, pretending they were defenders.

"I loved growing up in the mountains," he said. "We caught snakes, played in the woods."

Nance grew up in Anderson, a town in South Carolina's hill country not far from Clemson University. He grew up working on cars and loving stock car racing.

Dell Curry spent the 1987–88 season with the Cavaliers. The father of Stephen Curry, Dell grew up in Grottoes, Virginia. It's a small town in the Blue Ridge Mountains, not too far from Waynesboro. Hikers know Grottoes because you find a dirt road there leading to a trail into the hills that eventually reaches the Appalachian Trail. I've hiked that little, steep trail out of Grottoes. Curry's father set up a basketball hoop on an old utility pole. It was a gravel surface. That's where he learned to shoot.

Price grew up in suburban Enid, Oklahoma. His father was coaching at Phillips University, so he often practiced in that gym.

"But I remember being a 10-year-old shooting baskets in the driveway until it was too dark to see," said Price. "My mom would yell at me to come into the house. I'd tell her to wait five more minutes. Those were the days. Just me . . . a ball . . . and a basket."

Craig Ehlo was from Lubbock, Texas. Tree Rollins was from Cordele, Georgia. Ron Harper was from Dayton, Ohio.

Nearly all the players lived in Summit County, not far from Akron. That's because it was close to the Coliseum.

Coach Lenny Wilkens and guard Mark Price talk strategy on the sidelines.
Curt Chandler / The Plain Dealer

"We went to each other's houses a lot," said Price. "There was an immediate connection."

*   *   *

General manager Wayne Embry carefully picked the roster. He stressed the high character of players. He was criticized for having a team that was "soft" physically. This was during the "Bad Boys" Era in Detroit when the Pistons were shoving, holding and body-slamming opponents.

In the late 1980s, Detroit dominated in the Eastern Conference. The Bulls didn't win their first title until 1991.

The Pistons would not be able to play such a physical and often dirty style in the modern NBA. Years ago, the league mandated the officials to call the game tighter. The goal was to create more opportunities for the beautiful side of basketball—the shooting, passing and drives to the rim for layups and dunks. In the late 1980s, the Pistons "Bad Boys" approach was marketed by the franchise and the league. Embry was outraged when one of the NBA's highlight videos featured the Pistons knocking opposing players to the court.

On Feb. 28, 1989, Detroit's Rick Mahorn ran down the court and whacked Price in the side of the head with an elbow. Price didn't have the ball. In fact, the ball was about 40 feet from the play. It was evident Mahorn wanted to knock Price out of the game, and he did. Price suffered a concussion.

Today, Mahorn would be suspended for several games. Back then, he was fined $5,000, but no suspension. It was a very dangerous play.

Embry was right. They were selling violence, much like hockey fights. The league eventually came around to Embry's thinking. But in the late 1980s, it sounded as if Embry was whining because the Cavs couldn't beat the Pistons. The Chicago Bulls were making the same charges against Detroit. They were worried Jordan would suffer a major injury when facing Detroit.

I recall the Cavs being ripped for playing "pretty basketball."

What was wrong with basketball that stressed passing, ball-handling and shooting skills? The Cavs were among the league leaders in blocked shots with Nance and Williams. Even their defense had an artsy feel to it because those two Cavs big men had such wonderful timing as they blocked the shots.

The Cavs were like Lenny Wilkens. They were a smart, unselfish team. They had intricate out-of-bounds plays. They knew how to pass the ball to the low post. They understood the concept of "spacing," meaning players spreading out on both sides of the floor on offense. That made them harder to defend.

*   *   *

Danny Ferry has a unique perspective on the Cavaliers. He played for them from 1990-2000. He later became the general manager for the Cavs and the Atlanta Hawks.

His father was Bob Ferry, a former NBA center and general

manager. Ferry grew up when his father was drafting players and making trades for Washington's NBA franchise.

"The chemistry on those (Cavaliers) teams was so strong because they were people of high character," said Ferry. "Larry Nance was the kind of guy to bring everyone together. Larry and those guys accepted me when I came, and that meant so much to me."

Ferry never became the player the Cavs expected when they traded for him. He suffered a major knee injury playing in Italy. He ended up having five knee surgeries in his career.

"Those Cavs were unique because they had big players who also were skilled," said Ferry. "Back then, many of the 'Bigs' had no skill. They were there to give fouls, rebound and bang bodies under the basket. But Hot Rod, Nance and Daugherty were so skilled, so smart."

The 7-foot Daugherty played his last game for the Cavaliers in 1994 at the age of 28. His career was cut short by major back surgeries.

Daugherty made five All-Star teams in his eight seasons. He averaged 19 points and 9.5 rebounds, shooting 53 percent from the field.

"I played with Tim Duncan (in San Antonio) and Brad at his best had some similarities to Duncan," said Ferry. "He was such a fundamentally sound big man."

The 6-foot-10 Ferry played against Williams, Nance and Daugherty often in practice.

"Hot Rod was a freak, especially on defense," said Ferry, explaining how the 6-foot-11 Williams could defend guards, forwards and centers.

"He was amazing defensively, and he could score if they needed him to do that," said Ferry.

Like Williams, the 6-foot-10 Nance was a shot blocker. He developed into a solid medium-range jump shooter. He made two All-Star teams with Cavs.

"All of those guys would have value in today's game," said Ferry. "Now, big men take 3-pointers. Those guys could learn to do that.

The Cavs had Price, Craig Ehlo and Steve (Kerr) already shooting 3-pointers. With a few small adjustments, that team would win a lot of games in the modern NBA."

The Cavs of that era reached the NBA Eastern Conference Finals in 1992, defeating New Jersey and the Boston Celtics in the first two rounds. They were eliminated by the Bulls in a six-game series. In the Lenny Wilkens Era, they made the playoffs every year from 1988 to 1993 with the exception of 1991. That season, Price tore the ACL in his knee and played only 16 games.

But the playoffs were frustrating because of Michael Jordan and the Bulls.

"The other tough part for the Cavs was they often had injuries in the postseason," said Ferry. "But it seemed the Bulls almost never did. Look it up. Jordan, Pippen and those guys always were healthy."

Price talked about "missing" those Richfield Coliseum times.

"I recently went out to where the Coliseum used to be," said Price. "It's just a field. It's just gone. It's almost like that part of my life didn't happen."

But it did happen, as many of you reading this book know.

Maybe you were a fan of the Miracle of Richfield Cavaliers. Maybe you have a soft spot in your heart for the first few Cavalier teams.

None of them won titles. But they were teams and players that take us back to a certain time and place—be it the old Cleveland Arena or the then sparkling new Richfield Coliseum.

For many of us, that's good enough.